# Mastering 11+
## Cloze
## Exercise Book 2

**ISBN: 1502918552**
**ISBN-13: 978-1502918550**

References: The Project Gutenbert Ebooks:
Brothers of Pity & Other tales of Beasts and men by Juliana Horatia Ewing
The Blue Fairy Book by Various (Edited by Andrew Lang)
Night Sketches by Nathaniel Hawthorne
The Little Lame Prince by Dinah Maria Mulock Craik and Margaret Waters
Eric and Sally by Johanna Spyri
Treasure Island by Robert Louis Stevenson
Black Beauty by Anna Sewell

Imprint id: M11PLUS/Cloze/20150717/1

## DEDICATION

To all children preparing for the eleven plus exams and
the parents who want nothing but the best for their kids.

> "Success is where preparation and
> opportunity meet."
>
> **Bobby Unser**

# Mastering 11+
# Cloze
## Practice Book 2

ashkraft
EDUCATIONAL

Mastering 11+ © 2015 ashkraft educational

*This page is intentionally left blank*

# Table of Contents

# WORD MATCHING

## EXERCISE 1:

**Instructions: For each question in the following passage, select the most appropriate word from the table below.**

| A. one | B. allowed | C. backs | D. shelves | E. better |
|--------|-----------|----------|-----------|-----------|
| F. except | G. persuade | H. books | I. belong | J. reading |

It must be much easier to play at things when there are more of you than when there is only

**1** [_____] .

There is only one of me, and Nurse does not care about playing at things. Sometimes I try to

**2** [_____] her; but if she is in a good temper she says she has got a bone in her

leg, and if she isn't she says that when little boys can't amuse themselves it's a sure and

certain sign they've got "the worrits," and the sooner they are put to bed with a Gregory's

powder "the **3** [_____] for themselves and everyone else."

Godfather Gilpin can play delightfully when he has time, and he believes in fancy things, only

he is so very busy with his books. But even when he is **4** [_____] he will let

you put him in the game. He doesn't mind pretending to be a fancy person if he hasn't to do anything, and if I do speak to him he always remembers who he is. That is why I like playing

in his study better than in the nursery. And Nurse always says "He's safe enough, with the old

gentleman," so I'm [ 5 ] to go there as much as I like.

Godfather Gilpin lets me play with the books, because I always take care of them. Besides,

there is nothing else to play with, [ 6 ] the window-curtains, for the

chairs are always full. So I sit on the floor, and sometimes I build with the books (particularly

Stonehenge), and sometimes I make people of them, and call them by the names on their

[ 7 ] , and the ones in other languages we call foreigners, and Godfather

Gilpin tells me what countries they [ 8 ] to. And sometimes I lie on my

face and read (for I could read when I was four years old), and Godfather Gilpin tells me the

hard words. The only rule he makes is, that I must get all the [ 9 ] out

of one shelf, so that they are easily put away again. I may have any shelf I like, but I must not

mix the [ 10 ] up.

**Exercise 1 - Answer Sheet:**

| | A | B | C | D | E | F | G | H | I | J |
|---|---|---|---|---|---|---|---|---|---|---|
| **1** | ☐ | ☐ | ☐ | ☐ | ☐ | ☐ | ☐ | ☐ | ☐ | ☐ |
| **2** | ☐ | ☐ | ☐ | ☐ | ☐ | ☐ | ☐ | ☐ | ☐ | ☐ |
| **3** | ☐ | ☐ | ☐ | ☐ | ☐ | ☐ | ☐ | ☐ | ☐ | ☐ |
| **4** | ☐ | ☐ | ☐ | ☐ | ☐ | ☐ | ☐ | ☐ | ☐ | ☐ |
| **5** | ☐ | ☐ | ☐ | ☐ | ☐ | ☐ | ☐ | ☐ | ☐ | ☐ |
| **6** | ☐ | ☐ | ☐ | ☐ | ☐ | ☐ | ☐ | ☐ | ☐ | ☐ |
| **7** | ☐ | ☐ | ☐ | ☐ | ☐ | ☐ | ☐ | ☐ | ☐ | ☐ |
| **8** | ☐ | ☐ | ☐ | ☐ | ☐ | ☐ | ☐ | ☐ | ☐ | ☐ |
| **9** | ☐ | ☐ | ☐ | ☐ | ☐ | ☐ | ☐ | ☐ | ☐ | ☐ |
| **10** | ☐ | ☐ | ☐ | ☐ | ☐ | ☐ | ☐ | ☐ | ☐ | ☐ |

## EXERCISE 2:

**Instructions: For each question in the following passage, select the most appropriate word from the table below.**

| A. | know | B. | finished | C. | preach | D. | happened | E. | against |
|----|------|----|----------|----|--------|----|----------|----|---------|
| F. | congregation | G. | books | H. | hymns | I. | find | J. | sounded |

It [ **1** ] on a Sunday, I remember, and it was the day after the day on

which I had had the shelf in which all the books were alike. They were all foreigners—

Italians—and all their names were *Goldoni*, and there were forty-seven of them, and they

were all in white and gold. I could not read any of them, but there were lots of pictures, only

I did not [ **2** ] what the stories were about. So next day, when Godfather

Gilpin gave me leave to play a Sunday game with the [ **3** ] , I thought I

would have English ones, and big ones, for a change, for the *Goldonis* were rather small.

We played at church, and I was the parson, and Godfather Gilpin was the old gentleman who

sits in the big pew with the knocker, and goes to sleep (because he wanted to go to sleep),

and the books were the [ **4** ] . They were all big, but some of them

were fat, and some of them were thin, like real people—not like the *Goldonis*, which were all

Mastering 11+/Cloze – Book TWO/ashkraft educational

alike.

I was arranging them in their places and looking at their names, when I saw that one of them was called Taylor's *Sermons*, and I thought I would keep that one out and [ 5 _____ ] a real sermon out of it when I had read prayers. Of course I had to do the responses as well as "Dearly beloved brethren" and those things, and I had to sing the [ 6 _____ ] too, for the books could not do anything, and Godfather Gilpin was asleep.

When I had [ 7 _____ ] the service I stood behind a chair that was full of newspapers, for a pulpit, and I lifted up Taylor's *Sermons*, and rested it [ 8 _____ ] the chair, and began to look to see what I would preach. It was an old book, bound in brown leather, and ornamented with gold, with a picture of a man in a black gown and a round black cap and a white collar in the beginning; and there was a list of all the sermons with their names and the texts. I read it through, to see which [ 9 _____ ] the most interesting, and I didn't care much for any of them. However, the last but one was called "A Funeral Sermon, preached at the Obsequies of the Right Honourable the Countess of Carbery;" and I wondered what obsequies were, and who the Countess of Carbery was, and I thought I would preach that sermon and try to [ 10 _____ ] out.

**Exercise 2 - Answer Sheet:**

| 1 | A ▭ | B ▭ | C ▭ | D ▭ | E ▭ | F ▭ | G ▭ | H ▭ | I ▭ | J ▭ |
| 2 | A ▭ | B ▭ | C ▭ | D ▭ | E ▭ | F ▭ | G ▭ | H ▭ | I ▭ | J ▭ |
| 3 | A ▭ | B ▭ | C ▭ | D ▭ | E ▭ | F ▭ | G ▭ | H ▭ | I ▭ | J ▭ |
| 4 | A ▭ | B ▭ | C ▭ | D ▭ | E ▭ | F ▭ | G ▭ | H ▭ | I ▭ | J ▭ |
| 5 | A ▭ | B ▭ | C ▭ | D ▭ | E ▭ | F ▭ | G ▭ | H ▭ | I ▭ | J ▭ |
| 6 | A ▭ | B ▭ | C ▭ | D ▭ | E ▭ | F ▭ | G ▭ | H ▭ | I ▭ | J ▭ |
| 7 | A ▭ | B ▭ | C ▭ | D ▭ | E ▭ | F ▭ | G ▭ | H ▭ | I ▭ | J ▭ |
| 8 | A ▭ | B ▭ | C ▭ | D ▭ | E ▭ | F ▭ | G ▭ | H ▭ | I ▭ | J ▭ |
| 9 | A ▭ | B ▭ | C ▭ | D ▭ | E ▭ | F ▭ | G ▭ | H ▭ | I ▭ | J ▭ |
| 10 | A ▭ | B ▭ | C ▭ | D ▭ | E ▭ | F ▭ | G ▭ | H ▭ | I ▭ | J ▭ |

Mastering 11+/Cloze – Book TWO/ashkraft educational

EXERCISE 3:

Instructions: For each question in the following passage, select the most appropriate word from the table below.

| A. imaginable | B. father | C. twilight | D. taste | E. throat |
|---|---|---|---|---|
| F. opposite | G. sun | H. pasture | I. children | J. fear |

That summer—I mean the summer when I had seven—we had the most charming home

**1** [ ] . It was in a wood, and on that side of the wood which is farthest

from houses and highroads. Here it was bounded by a brook, and beyond this lay a fine

**2** [ ] field.

There are fields and fields. I never wish to know a better field than this one. I seldom go out

much till the evening, but if business should take one along the hedge in the heat of the

**3** [ ] , there are as juicy and refreshing crabs to be picked up under a tree

about half-way down the south side, as the thirstiest creature could desire.

And when the glare and drought of midday have given place to the mild **4** [ ] of

evening, and the grass is refreshingly damped with dew, and scents are strong, and the earth

yields kindly to the nose, what beetles and lob-worms reward one's routing!

I am convinced that the fattest and stupidest slugs that live, live near the brook. I never knew

one who found out I was eating him, till he was half-way down my [ 5 _____ ].

And just [ 6 _____ ] to the place where I furnished your dear mother's nest, is a

small plantation of burdocks, on the underside of which stick the best flavoured snails I am

acquainted with, in such inexhaustible quantities, that a hedgehog might have fourteen

children in a season, and not [ 7 _____ ] their coming short of provisions.

My dear children, my seven dear children, may you never know what it is to taste a

pheasant's egg—to taste several pheasant's eggs, and to [ 8 _____ ] them,

shells and all.

There are certain pleasures of which a parent may himself have partaken, but which, if he

cannot reconcile them with his ideas of safety and propriety, he will do well not to allow his

[ 9 _____ ] even to hear of. I do not say that I wish I had never tasted a

pheasant's egg myself, but, when I think of traps baited with valerian, of my great-uncle's

great-coat nailed to the keeper's door, of the keeper's heavy-heeled boots, and of the

impropriety of poaching, I feel, as a [ 10 _____ ], that it is desirable that you

should never know that there are such things as eggs, and then you will be quite happy

without them.

**Exercise 3 - Answer Sheet:**

| 1 | A | B | C | D | E | F | G | H | I | J |
|---|---|---|---|---|---|---|---|---|---|---|
| **1** | A ▭ | B ▭ | C ▭ | D ▭ | E ▭ | F ▭ | G ▭ | H ▭ | I ▭ | J ▭ |
| **2** | A ▭ | B ▭ | C ▭ | D ▭ | E ▭ | F ▭ | G ▭ | H ▭ | I ▭ | J ▭ |
| **3** | A ▭ | B ▭ | C ▭ | D ▭ | E ▭ | F ▭ | G ▭ | H ▭ | I ▭ | J ▭ |
| **4** | A ▭ | B ▭ | C ▭ | D ▭ | E ▭ | F ▭ | G ▭ | H ▭ | I ▭ | J ▭ |
| **5** | A ▭ | B ▭ | C ▭ | D ▭ | E ▭ | F ▭ | G ▭ | H ▭ | I ▭ | J ▭ |
| **6** | A ▭ | B ▭ | C ▭ | D ▭ | E ▭ | F ▭ | G ▭ | H ▭ | I ▭ | J ▭ |
| **7** | A ▭ | B ▭ | C ▭ | D ▭ | E ▭ | F ▭ | G ▭ | H ▭ | I ▭ | J ▭ |
| **8** | A ▭ | B ▭ | C ▭ | D ▭ | E ▭ | F ▭ | G ▭ | H ▭ | I ▭ | J ▭ |
| **9** | A ▭ | B ▭ | C ▭ | D ▭ | E ▭ | F ▭ | G ▭ | H ▭ | I ▭ | J ▭ |
| **10** | A ▭ | B ▭ | C ▭ | D ▭ | E ▭ | F ▭ | G ▭ | H ▭ | I ▭ | J ▭ |

## EXERCISE 4:

**Instructions: For each question in the following passage, select the most appropriate word from the table below.**

| A. time | B. cream | C. slightest | D. shutting | E. ungrateful |
|---------|----------|--------------|-------------|---------------|
| F. blast | G. heard | H. inward | I. saucers | J. supposed |

My name is Toots. Why, I have not the [ **1** ] idea. But I suppose very few

people—cats or otherwise—are consulted about their own names. If they were, these would

perhaps be, as a rule, more appropriate.

What qualities of mind or body my name was [ **2** ] to illustrate, I have not

to this hour a notion. I distinctly remember the stage of my kittenhood, when I thought that

Toots was the English for cream.

"Toots! Toots!" my young mistress used to say, in the most suggestive tones, creeping after

me as I would creep after a mouse, with a saucerful of that delicious liquid in her hand.

"Toots is first-rate stuff," I used to think, and I purred accordingly, for I never was an

[ **3** ] cat.

This was in the dining-room, and in the morning. Later in the day, "Toots" was served in the

Mastering 11+/Cloze – Book TWO/ashkraft educational

drawing-room. It was between these two periods, I remember, that one day I found myself in the larder. Why I went there, puzzled me at the [ 4 ] ; for if there is anything I hate it is a chill, and there was a horrid draught through a window pierced with tiny holes, which seemed to let in a separate [ 5 ] for every hair of one's fur. I followed the cook, it is true; but I did not follow the cook as a rule—not, for instance, when she went out to the coal-hole in the yard. I had slipped in under her dress. I was behind the potato-tub when she went out, [ 6 ] the door after her.

For some mysterious reason I felt on the tip-claw of expectation. My nose twitched with agreeable sensations. An [ 7 ] voice seemed to murmur, *Toots*!

Regardless of the draughts, I sprang on to the shelf close under the window. And there was such a dish of cream! The [ 8 ] in which one got it at breakfast did not hold a twentieth part of what this brimming pan contained. As to the five o'clock china, in which visitors give you a tepid teaspoonful, with bits of old tea-leaves in it—I grinned at the thought as I drew in tongueful after tongueful of the thick yellow [ 9 ].

At this moment I [ 10 ] my young mistress's voice in the distant passages.

**Exercise 4 - Answer Sheet:**

| | A | B | C | D | E | F | G | H | I | J |
|---|---|---|---|---|---|---|---|---|---|---|
| **1** | ☐ | ☐ | ☐ | ☐ | ☐ | ☐ | ☐ | ☐ | ☐ | ☐ |
| **2** | ☐ | ☐ | ☐ | ☐ | ☐ | ☐ | ☐ | ☐ | ☐ | ☐ |
| **3** | ☐ | ☐ | ☐ | ☐ | ☐ | ☐ | ☐ | ☐ | ☐ | ☐ |
| **4** | ☐ | ☐ | ☐ | ☐ | ☐ | ☐ | ☐ | ☐ | ☐ | ☐ |
| **5** | ☐ | ☐ | ☐ | ☐ | ☐ | ☐ | ☐ | ☐ | ☐ | ☐ |
| **6** | ☐ | ☐ | ☐ | ☐ | ☐ | ☐ | ☐ | ☐ | ☐ | ☐ |
| **7** | ☐ | ☐ | ☐ | ☐ | ☐ | ☐ | ☐ | ☐ | ☐ | ☐ |
| **8** | ☐ | ☐ | ☐ | ☐ | ☐ | ☐ | ☐ | ☐ | ☐ | ☐ |
| **9** | ☐ | ☐ | ☐ | ☐ | ☐ | ☐ | ☐ | ☐ | ☐ | ☐ |
| **10** | ☐ | ☐ | ☐ | ☐ | ☐ | ☐ | ☐ | ☐ | ☐ | ☐ |

## EXERCISE 5:

Instructions: For each question in the following passage, select the most appropriate word from the table below.

| A. responding | B. seemed | C. claws | D. understand | E. drop |
|---|---|---|---|---|
| F. shelter | G. opened | H. chased | I. confused | J. whip |

"Toots, Toots!" snapped the cook.

"Miow," said I; for I had finished the cream, and could speak now, though I confess I did not feel equal to any great exertion.

The cook [ **1** ] the door. She found me—she did not find the cream, which she had left in the dish ready for whipping.

Perhaps it was because she had no cream to whip, that she tried to [ **2** ] me. Certainly, during the next half-hour, I had reason to be much [ **3** ] as to the meaning of the word "Toots." In the soft voice of my mistress it had always seemed to me to mean cream; now it [ **4** ] to mean kicks, blows, flapping dish-cloths, wash-leathers and dusters, pokers, carpet brooms, and every instrument of torture with which a poor cat could be [ **5** ] from garret to cellar. I am pretty nimble, and though I never felt less disposed for violent exercise, I flatter myself I led them a

good dance before, by a sudden impulse of affectionate trustfulness, I sprang straight into

my mistress's arms for [ 6 _____ ] .

"You must beat him, miss," gasped the cook, "or there'll never be no bearing him in the

house. Every [ 7 _____ ] of that lovely cream gone, and half the sweets for the

ball supper throwed completely out of calculation!"

"Naughty Toots, naughty Toots, naughty Toots!" cried the young lady, and with every "Toots"

she gave me a slap; but as her paws had no [ 8 _____ ] in them, I was more

offended than hurt.

This was my first lesson in honesty, and it was also the beginning of that train of reasoning in

my own mind, by which I came to [ 9 _____ ] that when people called "Toots"

they meant me. And as—to do them justice—they generally called me with some kind

intention, I made a point of [ 10 _____ ] to my name.

**Exercise 5 - Answer Sheet:**

| 1 | A | B | C | D | E | F | G | H | I | J |
|---|---|---|---|---|---|---|---|---|---|---|
| **1** | ☐ | ☐ | ☐ | ☐ | ☐ | ☐ | ☐ | ☐ | ☐ | ☐ |
| **2** | ☐ | ☐ | ☐ | ☐ | ☐ | ☐ | ☐ | ☐ | ☐ | ☐ |
| **3** | ☐ | ☐ | ☐ | ☐ | ☐ | ☐ | ☐ | ☐ | ☐ | ☐ |
| **4** | ☐ | ☐ | ☐ | ☐ | ☐ | ☐ | ☐ | ☐ | ☐ | ☐ |
| **5** | ☐ | ☐ | ☐ | ☐ | ☐ | ☐ | ☐ | ☐ | ☐ | ☐ |
| **6** | ☐ | ☐ | ☐ | ☐ | ☐ | ☐ | ☐ | ☐ | ☐ | ☐ |
| **7** | ☐ | ☐ | ☐ | ☐ | ☐ | ☐ | ☐ | ☐ | ☐ | ☐ |
| **8** | ☐ | ☐ | ☐ | ☐ | ☐ | ☐ | ☐ | ☐ | ☐ | ☐ |
| **9** | ☐ | ☐ | ☐ | ☐ | ☐ | ☐ | ☐ | ☐ | ☐ | ☐ |
| **10** | ☐ | ☐ | ☐ | ☐ | ☐ | ☐ | ☐ | ☐ | ☐ | ☐ |

EXERCISE 6:

_____

Instructions: For each question in the following passage, select the most appropriate word from the table below.

| A. undisputed | B. hottest | C. hens | D. shade | E. sleep |
|---|---|---|---|---|
| F. plenty | G. glare | H. carry | I. glistened | J. dead |

What a hot, drowsy afternoon it was.

The blazing sun shone with such a **1** [_____] upon the farmyard that it was

almost unbearable, and there was not a vestige of grass or any green thing to relieve the eye

or cast a little **2** [_____].

But the fowls in the back yard were not disturbed by the heat the least bit in the world, for

they had **3** [_____] of time in which to doze, and they were fond of taking a

siesta in the hottest place that could be found. Certainly the **4** [_____] place

that afternoon, by far, was the yard in which they reposed.

There were five of them—a cock and four hens. Two of the **5** [_____] were

renowned throughout the whole village, for they wore tufts of feathers on their heads

Mastering 11+/Cloze – Book TWO/ashkraft educational

instead of the usual red combs; and the cock was very proud of having such distinguished-

looking wives.

Besides which, he was naturally a very stately bird himself in appearance, and had a splendid

blackish-green tail and a golden speckled hackle, which shone and [ 6 _____ ] in

the sun. He had also won many sharp battles with certain young cocks in the neighbourhood,

whom curiosity about the tufted foreigners had attracted to the yard. The consequence of

these triumphs was that he held [ 7 _____ ] dominion as far as the second

fence from the farmyard, and whenever he shut his eyes and sounded his war-clarion, the

whole of his rivals made off as fast as wings and legs could [ 8 _____ ] them.

So the five sat or stood by themselves in the yard, dozing in the sunshine, and they felt

bored.

During the middle of the day they had managed to get some winks of [ 9 _____ ],

but now the farmer's men began to thresh in a barn close by, making noise enough to wake

the [ 10 _____ ] , so there was small chance of well-organized fowls being able

to sleep through the din.

**Exercise 6 - Answer Sheet:**

| 1 | A | B | C | D | E | F | G | H | I | J |
|---|---|---|---|---|---|---|---|---|---|---|
| 2 | A | B | C | D | E | F | G | H | I | J |
| 3 | A | B | C | D | E | F | G | H | I | J |
| 4 | A | B | C | D | E | F | G | H | I | J |
| 5 | A | B | C | D | E | F | G | H | I | J |
| 6 | A | B | C | D | E | F | G | H | I | J |
| 7 | A | B | C | D | E | F | G | H | I | J |
| 8 | A | B | C | D | E | F | G | H | I | J |
| 9 | A | B | C | D | E | F | G | H | I | J |
| 10 | A | B | C | D | E | F | G | H | I | J |

Mastering 11+/Cloze – Book TWO/ashkraft educational

## EXERCISE 7:

**Instructions: For each question in the following passage, select the most appropriate word from the table below.**

| A. class | B. beyond | C. sorry | D. obstinate | E. bore |
|----------|-----------|----------|--------------|---------|
| F. content | G. beginning | H. live | I. intelligence | J. moral |

Very few beetles have ever seen a Glass Pond. I once spent a week in one, and though I think, with good management, and in society suitably selected, it may be a comfortable home enough, I advise my water-neighbours to be ☐ **1** ☐ with the pond in the wood.

The story of my brief sojourn in the Glass Pond is a story with a ☐ **2** ☐ , and it concerns two large classes of my fellow-creatures: those who live in ponds and—those who don't. If I do not tell it, no one else will. Those connected with it who belong to the second ☐ **3** ☐ (namely, Francis, Molly, and the learned Doctor, their grandfather) will not, I am sure. And as to the rest of us, there is none left but—

However, that is the end of my tale, not the ☐ **4** ☐ .

The beginning, as far as I am concerned, was in the Pond. It is very difficult to describe a

pond to people who cannot [ 5 ] under water, just as I found it next

door to impossible to make a minnow I knew believe in dry land. He said, at last, that

perhaps there might be some little space beyond the pond in hot weather, when the water

was low; and that was the utmost that he would allow. But of all cold-blooded

unconvinceable creatures, the most [ 6 ] are fish.

Men are very different. They do not refuse to believe what lies [ 7 ] their

personal experience. I respected the learned Doctor, and was really sorry for the

disadvantages under which he laboured. That a creature of his [ 8 ]

should have only two eyes, and those not even compound ones—that he should not be able

to see under water or in the dark—that he should not only have nothing like six legs, but be

quite without wings, so that he could not even fly out of his own window for a turn in the air

on a summer's evening—these drawbacks made me quite [ 9 ] for him;

for he had none of the minnow's complacent ignorance. He knew my advantages as well as I

knew them myself, and [ 10 ] me no ill-will for them.

# Exercise 7 - Answer Sheet:

| | | | | | | | | | | |
|---|---|---|---|---|---|---|---|---|---|---|
| **1** | A ▭ | B ▭ | C ▭ | D ▭ | E ▭ | F ▭ | G ▭ | H ▭ | I ▭ | J ▭ |
| **2** | A ▭ | B ▭ | C ▭ | D ▭ | E ▭ | F ▭ | G ▭ | H ▭ | I ▭ | J ▭ |
| **3** | A ▭ | B ▭ | C ▭ | D ▭ | E ▭ | F ▭ | G ▭ | H ▭ | I ▭ | J ▭ |
| **4** | A ▭ | B ▭ | C ▭ | D ▭ | E ▭ | F ▭ | G ▭ | H ▭ | I ▭ | J ▭ |
| **5** | A ▭ | B ▭ | C ▭ | D ▭ | E ▭ | F ▭ | G ▭ | H ▭ | I ▭ | J ▭ |
| **6** | A ▭ | B ▭ | C ▭ | D ▭ | E ▭ | F ▭ | G ▭ | H ▭ | I ▭ | J ▭ |
| **7** | A ▭ | B ▭ | C ▭ | D ▭ | E ▭ | F ▭ | G ▭ | H ▭ | I ▭ | J ▭ |
| **8** | A ▭ | B ▭ | C ▭ | D ▭ | E ▭ | F ▭ | G ▭ | H ▭ | I ▭ | J ▭ |
| **9** | A ▭ | B ▭ | C ▭ | D ▭ | E ▭ | F ▭ | G ▭ | H ▭ | I ▭ | J ▭ |
| **10** | A ▭ | B ▭ | C ▭ | D ▭ | E ▭ | F ▭ | G ▭ | H ▭ | I ▭ | J ▭ |

## EXERCISE 8:

Instructions: For each question in the following passage, select the most appropriate word from the table below.

| A. noticed | B. address | C. also | D. bright | E. help |
|---|---|---|---|---|
| F. give | G. behind | H. explain | I. meditating | J. awake |

I am an Owl; a very fluffy one, in spite of all that that Bad Boy pulled out! I live in an Ivy Bush.

Children are nothing to me, naturally, so it seems strange that I should begin, at my time of

life, to observe their little ways and their humours, and to [ **1** ] them

good advice.

And yet it is so. I am the Friend of Young People. In my flight abroad I watch them. As I sit

[ **2** ] in my Ivy Bush, it is their little matters which I turn over in my fluffy

head. I have established a letter-box for their communications at the Hole in the Tree. No

other [ **3** ] will find me.

It is well known that I am a Bird of Wisdom. I am [ **4** ] an Observing

Bird; and though my young friends may think I see less than I do, because of my blinking, and

because I detest that vulgar glare of [ **5** ] light without which some persons do not seem able to see what goes on around them, I would have children to know

that if I can blink on occasion, and am not apt to let every starer read my counsel in my eyes,

I am wide [ **6** _____ ] all the same. I am on the look-out when it's so dark that

other folk can't see an inch before their noses, and (a word to the foolish and naughty!) I can

see what is doing [ **7** _____ ] my back. And Wiseacre, Observer, and Wide-

awake—I am the Children's Owl.

Before I open my mouth on their little affairs, before even I open my letters (if there are any

waiting for me) I will [ **8** _____ ] how it came about that I am the Children's

Owl.

It is all owing to that little girl; the one with the fluffy hair and the wise eyes. As an Observer I

have [ **9** _____ ] that not only I, but other people, seem to do what she wants,

and as a Wiseacre I have reflected upon it as strange, because her temper is as soft and fluffy

as her hair (which mine is not), and she always seems ready to give way to others (which is

never my case—if I can help it). On the occasion I am about to speak of, I could *not*

[ **10** _____ ] it.

**Exercise 8 - Answer Sheet:**

| 1 | A ▭ | B ▭ | C ▭ | D ▭ | E ▭ | F ▭ | G ▭ | H ▭ | I ▭ | J ▭ |
| --- | --- | --- | --- | --- | --- | --- | --- | --- | --- | --- |
| 2 | A ▭ | B ▭ | C ▭ | D ▭ | E ▭ | F ▭ | G ▭ | H ▭ | I ▭ | J ▭ |
| 3 | A ▭ | B ▭ | C ▭ | D ▭ | E ▭ | F ▭ | G ▭ | H ▭ | I ▭ | J ▭ |
| 4 | A ▭ | B ▭ | C ▭ | D ▭ | E ▭ | F ▭ | G ▭ | H ▭ | I ▭ | J ▭ |
| 5 | A ▭ | B ▭ | C ▭ | D ▭ | E ▭ | F ▭ | G ▭ | H ▭ | I ▭ | J ▭ |
| 6 | A ▭ | B ▭ | C ▭ | D ▭ | E ▭ | F ▭ | G ▭ | H ▭ | I ▭ | J ▭ |
| 7 | A ▭ | B ▭ | C ▭ | D ▭ | E ▭ | F ▭ | G ▭ | H ▭ | I ▭ | J ▭ |
| 8 | A ▭ | B ▭ | C ▭ | D ▭ | E ▭ | F ▭ | G ▭ | H ▭ | I ▭ | J ▭ |
| 9 | A ▭ | B ▭ | C ▭ | D ▭ | E ▭ | F ▭ | G ▭ | H ▭ | I ▭ | J ▭ |
| 10 | A ▭ | B ▭ | C ▭ | D ▭ | E ▭ | F ▭ | G ▭ | H ▭ | I ▭ | J ▭ |

**Instructions: For each question in the following passage, select the most appropriate word from the table below.**

| A. show | B. large | C. real | D. endurance | E. running |
|---------|----------|---------|--------------|------------|
| F. pepper | G. cage | H. hoarse | I. feathers | J. caught |

It was last summer that that Bad Boy caught me, and squeezed me into a wicker cage. Little

did I think I should ever live to be so poked out, and rummaged, and torn to shreds by such a

thing as a boy! I bit him, but he got me into the [ 1 _____ ] and put a cloth

over it. Then he took me to his father, who took me to the front door of the house, where he

is coachman and gardener, and asked for Little Miss to come out and see the new pet Tom

had [ 2 _____ ] for her.

"It's a nasty-tempered brute, but she's such a one for taming things," said the coachman,

whipping off the cloth to [ 3 _____ ] me to the housemaid, and letting in a

glare of light that irritated me to a frenzy. I flew at the housemaid, and she flew into the

house. Then I rolled over and growled and hissed under my beak, and tried to hide my eyes

in my [ 4 _____ ].

"Little Miss won't tame me," I muttered.

She did not try long. When she heard of me she came [ 5 ] out, the

wind blowing her fluffy hair about her face, and the sun shining on it. Fluffed out by the

wind, and changing colour in the light and shade, the hair down her back is not entirely

unlike the feathers of my own, though less sober perhaps in its tints. Like mine it makes a

small head look [ 6 ], and as she had big wise eyes, I have seen creatures

less like an owl than Little Miss. Her voice is not so [ 7 ] as mine. It is

clear and soft, as I heard when she spoke:

"Oh, *how* good of you! And how good of Tom! I do so love owls. I always get Mary to put the

silver owl by me at luncheon, though I am not allowed to eat [ 8 ].

And I have a brown owl, a china one, sitting on a book for a letter weight. He came from

Germany. And Captain Barton gave me an owl pencil-case on my birthday, because I liked

hearing about his real owl, but, oh, I never hoped I should have a [ 9 ]

owl of my very own. It *was* kind of Tom."

To hear that Bad Boy called kind was too much for [ 10 ], and I let them

see how savage I felt. If the wicker work had not been very strong the cage would not have

held me.

**Exercise 9 - Answer Sheet:**

| | A | B | C | D | E | F | G | H | I | J |
|---|---|---|---|---|---|---|---|---|---|---|
| **1** | ▭ | ▭ | ▭ | ▭ | ▭ | ▭ | ▭ | ▭ | ▭ | ▭ |
| **2** | ▭ | ▭ | ▭ | ▭ | ▭ | ▭ | ▭ | ▭ | ▭ | ▭ |
| **3** | ▭ | ▭ | ▭ | ▭ | ▭ | ▭ | ▭ | ▭ | ▭ | ▭ |
| **4** | ▭ | ▭ | ▭ | ▭ | ▭ | ▭ | ▭ | ▭ | ▭ | ▭ |
| **5** | ▭ | ▭ | ▭ | ▭ | ▭ | ▭ | ▭ | ▭ | ▭ | ▭ |
| **6** | ▭ | ▭ | ▭ | ▭ | ▭ | ▭ | ▭ | ▭ | ▭ | ▭ |
| **7** | ▭ | ▭ | ▭ | ▭ | ▭ | ▭ | ▭ | ▭ | ▭ | ▭ |
| **8** | ▭ | ▭ | ▭ | ▭ | ▭ | ▭ | ▭ | ▭ | ▭ | ▭ |
| **9** | ▭ | ▭ | ▭ | ▭ | ▭ | ▭ | ▭ | ▭ | ▭ | ▭ |
| **10** | ▭ | ▭ | ▭ | ▭ | ▭ | ▭ | ▭ | ▭ | ▭ | ▭ |

EXERCISE 10:

_____

**Instructions: For each question in the following passage, select the most appropriate word from the table below.**

| A. worth | B. pleased | C. losing | D. princess | E. faults |
|----------|-----------|-----------|-------------|-----------|
| F. world | G. poets | H. portrait | I. possible | J. dressed |

Once upon a time there lived a queen who had been the mother of a great many children,

and of them all only one daughter was left. But then *she* was [ **1** _____ ] at

least a thousand.

Her mother, who, since the death of the King, her father, had nothing in the world she cared

for so much as this little Princess, was so terribly afraid of [ **2** _____ ] her that

she quite spoiled her, and never tried to correct any of her [ **3** _____ ] . The

consequence was that this little person, who was as pretty as possible, and was one day to

wear a crown, grew up so proud and so much in love with her own beauty that she despised

everyone else in the [ **4** _____ ] .

The Queen, her mother, by her caresses and flatteries, helped to make her believe that there

was nothing too good for her. She was [ **5** _____ ] almost always in the prettiest frocks, as a fairy, or as a queen going out to hunt, and the ladies of the Court

followed her dressed as forest fairies.

And to make her more vain than ever the Queen caused her [ **6** _____ ] to

be taken by the cleverest painters and sent it to several neighbouring kings with whom she

was very friendly.

When they saw this portrait they fell in love with the [ **7** _____ ] —every

one of them, but upon each it had a different effect. One fell ill, one went quite crazy, and a

few of the luckiest set off to see her as soon as [ **8** _____ ] , but these poor

princes became her slaves the moment they set eyes on her.

Never has there been a gayer Court. Twenty delightful kings did everything they could think

of to make themselves agreeable, and after having spent ever so much money in giving a

single entertainment thought themselves very lucky if the Princess said "That's pretty."

All this admiration vastly [ **9** _____ ] the Queen. Not a day passed but she

received seven or eight thousand sonnets, and as many elegies, madrigals, and songs, which

were sent her by all the [ **10** _____ ] in the world.

**Exercise 10 - Answer Sheet:**

| | A | B | C | D | E | F | G | H | I | J |
|---|---|---|---|---|---|---|---|---|---|---|
| **1** | ▭ | ▭ | ▭ | ▭ | ▭ | ▭ | ▭ | ▭ | ▭ | ▭ |
| **2** | ▭ | ▭ | ▭ | ▭ | ▭ | ▭ | ▭ | ▭ | ▭ | ▭ |
| **3** | ▭ | ▭ | ▭ | ▭ | ▭ | ▭ | ▭ | ▭ | ▭ | ▭ |
| **4** | ▭ | ▭ | ▭ | ▭ | ▭ | ▭ | ▭ | ▭ | ▭ | ▭ |
| **5** | ▭ | ▭ | ▭ | ▭ | ▭ | ▭ | ▭ | ▭ | ▭ | ▭ |
| **6** | ▭ | ▭ | ▭ | ▭ | ▭ | ▭ | ▭ | ▭ | ▭ | ▭ |
| **7** | ▭ | ▭ | ▭ | ▭ | ▭ | ▭ | ▭ | ▭ | ▭ | ▭ |
| **8** | ▭ | ▭ | ▭ | ▭ | ▭ | ▭ | ▭ | ▭ | ▭ | ▭ |
| **9** | ▭ | ▭ | ▭ | ▭ | ▭ | ▭ | ▭ | ▭ | ▭ | ▭ |
| **10** | ▭ | ▭ | ▭ | ▭ | ▭ | ▭ | ▭ | ▭ | ▭ | ▭ |

EXERCISE 11:

Instructions: For each question in the following passage, select the most appropriate word from the table below.

| A. nightingale | B. Princess | C. sorry | D. hangings | E. muttered |
|---|---|---|---|---|
| F. christening | G. diamonds | H. either | I. purpose | J. fairies |

There were formerly a king and a queen, who were so sorry that they had no children; so

**1** [          ] that it cannot be expressed. They went to all the waters in the world;

vows, pilgrimages, all ways were tried, and all to no **2** [          ].

At last, however, the Queen had a daughter. There was a very fine christening; and the

**3** [          ] had for her god-mothers all the fairies they could find in the whole

kingdom (they found seven), that every one of them might give her a gift, as was the custom

of fairies in those days. By this means the Princess had all the perfections imaginable.

After the ceremonies of the **4** [          ] were over, all the company returned

to the King's palace, where was prepared a great feast for the fairies. There was placed

before every one of them a magnificent cover with a case of massive gold, wherein were a

spoon, knife, and fork, all of pure gold set with **5** [          ] and rubies. But as

they were all sitting down at table they saw come into the hall a very old fairy, whom they had not invited, because it was above fifty years since she had been out of a certain tower,

and she was believed to be [ **6** ] dead or enchanted.

The King ordered her a cover, but could not furnish her with a case of gold as the others,

because they had only seven made for the seven fairies. The old Fairy fancied she was

slighted, and [ **7** ] some threats between her teeth. One of the young

fairies who sat by her overheard how she grumbled; and, judging that she might give the

little Princess some unlucky gift, went, as soon as they rose from table, and hid herself

behind the [ **8** ] , that she might speak last, and repair, as much as she

could, the evil which the old Fairy might intend.

In the meanwhile all the [ **9** ] began to give their gifts to the Princess.

The youngest gave her for gift that she should be the most beautiful person in the world; the

next, that she should have the wit of an angel; the third, that she should have a wonderful

grace in everything she did; the fourth, that she should dance perfectly well; the fifth, that

she should sing like a [ **10** ] ; and the sixth, that she should play all kinds

of music to the utmost perfection.

## Exercise 11 - Answer Sheet:

| | A | B | C | D | E | F | G | H | I | J |
|---|---|---|---|---|---|---|---|---|---|---|
| **1** | ▭ | ▭ | ▭ | ▭ | ▭ | ▭ | ▭ | ▭ | ▭ | ▭ |
| **2** | ▭ | ▭ | ▭ | ▭ | ▭ | ▭ | ▭ | ▭ | ▭ | ▭ |
| **3** | ▭ | ▭ | ▭ | ▭ | ▭ | ▭ | ▭ | ▭ | ▭ | ▭ |
| **4** | ▭ | ▭ | ▭ | ▭ | ▭ | ▭ | ▭ | ▭ | ▭ | ▭ |
| **5** | ▭ | ▭ | ▭ | ▭ | ▭ | ▭ | ▭ | ▭ | ▭ | ▭ |
| **6** | ▭ | ▭ | ▭ | ▭ | ▭ | ▭ | ▭ | ▭ | ▭ | ▭ |
| **7** | ▭ | ▭ | ▭ | ▭ | ▭ | ▭ | ▭ | ▭ | ▭ | ▭ |
| **8** | ▭ | ▭ | ▭ | ▭ | ▭ | ▭ | ▭ | ▭ | ▭ | ▭ |
| **9** | ▭ | ▭ | ▭ | ▭ | ▭ | ▭ | ▭ | ▭ | ▭ | ▭ |
| **10** | ▭ | ▭ | ▭ | ▭ | ▭ | ▭ | ▭ | ▭ | ▭ | ▭ |

## EXERCISE 12:

**Instructions: For each question in the following passage, select the most appropriate word from the table below.**

| A. wound | B. Give | C. spinning | D. forbidden | E. help |
|----------|---------|-------------|--------------|---------|
| F. awake | G. hasty | H. spindle | I. hangings | J. daughter |

(Continued from previous exercise)

The old Fairy's turn coming next, with a head shaking more with spite than age, she said that the Princess should have her hand pierced with a spindle and die of the **[1]**.

This terrible gift made the whole company tremble, and everybody fell a-crying.

At this very instant the young Fairy came out from behind the **[2]**, and spake these words aloud:

"Assure yourselves, O King and Queen, that your **[3]** shall not die of this disaster. It is true, I have no power to undo entirely what my elder has done. The Princess shall indeed pierce her hand with a **[4]**; but, instead of dying, she shall only fall into a profound sleep, which shall last a hundred years, at the expiration of which a king's son shall come and **[5]** her."

The King, to avoid the misfortune foretold by the old Fairy, caused immediately proclamation to be made, whereby everybody was [ **6** _____ ] , on pain of death, to spin

with a distaff and spindle, or to have so much as any spindle in their houses. About fifteen or

sixteen years after, the King and Queen being gone to one of their houses of pleasure, the

young Princess happened one day to divert herself in running up and down the palace; when

going up from one apartment to another, she came into a little room on the top of the

tower, where a good old woman, alone, was [ **7** _____ ] with her spindle. This

good woman had never heard of the King's proclamation against spindles.

"What are you doing there, goody?" said the Princess.

"I am spinning, my pretty child," said the old woman, who did not know who she was.

"Ha!" said the Princess, "this is very pretty; how do you do it? [ **8** _____ ] it to

me, that I may see if I can do so."

She had no sooner taken it into her hand than, whether being very [ **9** _____ ] at

it, somewhat unhandy, or that the decree of the Fairy had so ordained it, it ran into her

hand, and she fell down in a swoon. The good old woman, not knowing very well what to do

in this affair, cried out for [ **10** _____ ] .

**Exercise 12 - Answer Sheet:**

| | A | B | C | D | E | F | G | H | I | J |
|---|---|---|---|---|---|---|---|---|---|---|
| **1** | ▭ | ▭ | ▭ | ▭ | ▭ | ▭ | ▭ | ▭ | ▭ | ▭ |
| **2** | ▭ | ▭ | ▭ | ▭ | ▭ | ▭ | ▭ | ▭ | ▭ | ▭ |
| **3** | ▭ | ▭ | ▭ | ▭ | ▭ | ▭ | ▭ | ▭ | ▭ | ▭ |
| **4** | ▭ | ▭ | ▭ | ▭ | ▭ | ▭ | ▭ | ▭ | ▭ | ▭ |
| **5** | ▭ | ▭ | ▭ | ▭ | ▭ | ▭ | ▭ | ▭ | ▭ | ▭ |
| **6** | ▭ | ▭ | ▭ | ▭ | ▭ | ▭ | ▭ | ▭ | ▭ | ▭ |
| **7** | ▭ | ▭ | ▭ | ▭ | ▭ | ▭ | ▭ | ▭ | ▭ | ▭ |
| **8** | ▭ | ▭ | ▭ | ▭ | ▭ | ▭ | ▭ | ▭ | ▭ | ▭ |
| **9** | ▭ | ▭ | ▭ | ▭ | ▭ | ▭ | ▭ | ▭ | ▭ | ▭ |
| **10** | ▭ | ▭ | ▭ | ▭ | ▭ | ▭ | ▭ | ▭ | ▭ | ▭ |

Mastering 11+/Cloze – Book TWO/ashkraft educational

EXERCISE 13:

Instructions: For each question in the following passage, select the most appropriate word from the table below.

| A. peasants | B. fortunate | C. recovering | D. direst | E. fancied |
|-------------|--------------|---------------|-----------|------------|
| F. beginning | G. possessed | H. extravagance | I. dismal | J. despair |

Once upon a time, in a very far-off country, there lived a merchant who had been so

**1** [      ] in all his undertakings that he was enormously rich. As he had,

however, six sons and six daughters, he found that his money was not too much to let them

all have everything they **2** [      ], as they were accustomed to do.

But one day a most unexpected misfortune befell them. Their house caught fire and was

speedily burnt to the ground, with all the splendid furniture, the books, pictures, gold, silver,

and precious goods it contained; and this was only the **3** [      ] of their

troubles. Their father, who had until this moment prospered in all ways, suddenly lost every

ship he had upon the sea, either by dint of pirates, shipwreck, or fire. Then he heard that his

clerks in distant countries, whom he trusted entirely, had proved unfaithful; and at last from

great wealth he fell into the **4** [      ] poverty.

All that he had left was a little house in a desolate place at least a hundred leagues from the town in which he had lived, and to this he was forced to retreat with his children, who were in [ 5 ___ ] at the idea of leading such a different life. Indeed, the daughters at first hoped that their friends, who had been so numerous while they were rich, would insist on their staying in their houses now they no longer [ 6 ___ ] one. But they soon found that they were left alone, and that their former friends even attributed their misfortunes to their own [ 7 ___ ], and showed no intention of offering them any help. So nothing was left for them but to take their departure to the cottage, which stood in the midst of a dark forest, and seemed to be the most [ 8 ___ ] place upon the face of the earth. As they were too poor to have any servants, the girls had to work hard, like [ 9 ___ ], and the sons, for their part, cultivated the fields to earn their living. Roughly clothed, and living in the simplest way, the girls regretted unceasingly the luxuries and amusements of their former life; only the youngest tried to be brave and cheerful. She had been as sad as anyone when misfortune overtook her father, but, soon [ 10 ___ ] her natural gaiety, she set to work to make the best of things, to amuse her father and brothers as well as she could, and to try to persuade her sisters to join her in dancing and singing.

Mastering 11+/Cloze – Book TWO/ashkraft educational

# Exercise 13 - Answer Sheet:

| | A | B | C | D | E | F | G | H | I | J |
|---|---|---|---|---|---|---|---|---|---|---|
| **1** | ▭ | ▭ | ▭ | ▭ | ▭ | ▭ | ▭ | ▭ | ▭ | ▭ |
| **2** | ▭ | ▭ | ▭ | ▭ | ▭ | ▭ | ▭ | ▭ | ▭ | ▭ |
| **3** | ▭ | ▭ | ▭ | ▭ | ▭ | ▭ | ▭ | ▭ | ▭ | ▭ |
| **4** | ▭ | ▭ | ▭ | ▭ | ▭ | ▭ | ▭ | ▭ | ▭ | ▭ |
| **5** | ▭ | ▭ | ▭ | ▭ | ▭ | ▭ | ▭ | ▭ | ▭ | ▭ |
| **6** | ▭ | ▭ | ▭ | ▭ | ▭ | ▭ | ▭ | ▭ | ▭ | ▭ |
| **7** | ▭ | ▭ | ▭ | ▭ | ▭ | ▭ | ▭ | ▭ | ▭ | ▭ |
| **8** | ▭ | ▭ | ▭ | ▭ | ▭ | ▭ | ▭ | ▭ | ▭ | ▭ |
| **9** | ▭ | ▭ | ▭ | ▭ | ▭ | ▭ | ▭ | ▭ | ▭ | ▭ |
| **10** | ▭ | ▭ | ▭ | ▭ | ▭ | ▭ | ▭ | ▭ | ▭ | ▭ |

# EXERCISE 14:

**Instructions: For each question in the following passage, select the most appropriate word from the table below.**

| A. fit | B. tranquillity | C. possible | D. cleverer | E. poverty |
|--------|-----------------|-------------|-------------|------------|
| F. fortune | G. inquiries | H. noticing | I. choose | J. recover |

(Continued from previous exercise)

But they would do nothing of the sort, and, because she was not as doleful as themselves,

they declared that this miserable life was all she was **1** [_____] for. But she

was really far prettier and **2** [_____] than they were; indeed, she was so

lovely that she was always called Beauty. After two years, when they were all beginning to

get used to their new life, something happened to disturb their **3** [_____].

Their father received the news that one of his ships, which he had believed to be lost, had

come safely into port with a rich cargo. All the sons and daughters at once thought that their

**4** [_____] was at an end, and wanted to set out directly for the town; but their

father, who was more prudent, begged them to wait a little, and, though it was harvest time,

and he could ill be spared, determined to go himself first, to make **5** [_____].

Only the youngest daughter had any doubt but that they would soon again be as rich as they

were before, or at least rich enough to live comfortably in some town where they would find amusement and gay companions once more. So they all loaded their father with

commissions for jewels and dresses which it would have taken a [ **6** _____ ] to

buy; only Beauty, feeling sure that it was of no use, did not ask for anything. Her father,

[ **7** _____ ] her silence, said: "And what shall I bring for you, Beauty?"

"The only thing I wish for is to see you come home safely," she answered.

But this only vexed her sisters, who fancied she was blaming them for having asked for such

costly things. Her father, however, was pleased, but as he thought that at her age she

certainly ought to like pretty presents, he told her to [ **8** _____ ] something.

"Well, dear father," she said, "as you insist upon it, I beg that you will bring me a rose. I have

not seen one since we came here, and I love them so much."

So the merchant set out and reached the town as quickly as [ **9** _____ ] , but

only to find that his former companions, believing him to be dead, had divided between

them the goods which the ship had brought; and after six months of trouble and expense he

found himself as poor as when he started, having been able to [ **10** _____ ]

only just enough to pay the cost of his journey.

## Exercise 14 - Answer Sheet:

| # | A | B | C | D | E | F | G | H | I | J |
|---|---|---|---|---|---|---|---|---|---|---|
| 1 | ▭ | ▭ | ▭ | ▭ | ▭ | ▭ | ▭ | ▭ | ▭ | ▭ |
| 2 | ▭ | ▭ | ▭ | ▭ | ▭ | ▭ | ▭ | ▭ | ▭ | ▭ |
| 3 | ▭ | ▭ | ▭ | ▭ | ▭ | ▭ | ▭ | ▭ | ▭ | ▭ |
| 4 | ▭ | ▭ | ▭ | ▭ | ▭ | ▭ | ▭ | ▭ | ▭ | ▭ |
| 5 | ▭ | ▭ | ▭ | ▭ | ▭ | ▭ | ▭ | ▭ | ▭ | ▭ |
| 6 | ▭ | ▭ | ▭ | ▭ | ▭ | ▭ | ▭ | ▭ | ▭ | ▭ |
| 7 | ▭ | ▭ | ▭ | ▭ | ▭ | ▭ | ▭ | ▭ | ▭ | ▭ |
| 8 | ▭ | ▭ | ▭ | ▭ | ▭ | ▭ | ▭ | ▭ | ▭ | ▭ |
| 9 | ▭ | ▭ | ▭ | ▭ | ▭ | ▭ | ▭ | ▭ | ▭ | ▭ |
| 10 | ▭ | ▭ | ▭ | ▭ | ▭ | ▭ | ▭ | ▭ | ▭ | ▭ |

# EXERCISE 15:

**Instructions: For each question in the following passage, select the most appropriate word from the table below.**

| A. book | B. author | C. summits | D. around | E. venture |
|---------|-----------|------------|-----------|------------|
| F. enough | G. camels | H. countries | I. appear | J. without |

Pleasant is a rainy winter's day, within doors! The best study for such a day, or the best amusement,—call it which you will,—is a [ **1** ] of travels, describing scenes the most unlike that sombre one, which is mistily presented through the windows. I have experienced, that fancy is then most successful in imparting distinct shapes and vivid colors to the objects which the [ **2** ] has spread upon his page, and that his words become magic spells to summon up a thousand varied pictures. Strange landscapes glimmer through the familiar walls of the room, and outlandish figures thrust themselves almost within the sacred precincts of the hearth. Small as my chamber is, it has space [ **3** ] to contain the ocean-like circumference of an Arabian desert, its parched sands tracked by the long line of a caravan, with the [ **4** ] patiently journeying through the heavy sunshine. Though my ceiling be not lofty, yet I can pile up the mountains of Central Asia beneath it, till their [5] shine far

above the clouds of the middle atmosphere. And, with my humble means, a wealth that is

not taxable, I can transport hither the magnificent merchandise of an Oriental bazaar, and

call a crowd of purchasers from distant [6] , to pay a fair profit for the

precious articles which are displayed on all sides. True it is, however, that amid the bustle of

traffic, or whatever else may seem to be going on [7] me, the rain-

drops will occasionally be heard to patter against my window-panes, which look forth upon

one of the quietest streets in a New England town. After a time, too, the visions vanish, and

will not [8] again at my bidding. Then, it being nightfall, a gloomy sense

of unreality depresses my spirits, and impels me to [9] out, before the

clock shall strike bedtime, to satisfy myself that the world is not entirely made up of such

shadowy materials, as have busied me throughout the day. A dreamer may dwell so long

among fantasies, that the things [10] him will seem as unreal as those

within.

**Exercise 15 - Answer Sheet:**

| | A | B | C | D | E | F | G | H | I | J |
|---|---|---|---|---|---|---|---|---|---|---|
| **1** | ▭ | ▭ | ▭ | ▭ | ▭ | ▭ | ▭ | ▭ | ▭ | ▭ |
| **2** | ▭ | ▭ | ▭ | ▭ | ▭ | ▭ | ▭ | ▭ | ▭ | ▭ |
| **3** | ▭ | ▭ | ▭ | ▭ | ▭ | ▭ | ▭ | ▭ | ▭ | ▭ |
| **4** | ▭ | ▭ | ▭ | ▭ | ▭ | ▭ | ▭ | ▭ | ▭ | ▭ |
| **5** | ▭ | ▭ | ▭ | ▭ | ▭ | ▭ | ▭ | ▭ | ▭ | ▭ |
| **6** | ▭ | ▭ | ▭ | ▭ | ▭ | ▭ | ▭ | ▭ | ▭ | ▭ |
| **7** | ▭ | ▭ | ▭ | ▭ | ▭ | ▭ | ▭ | ▭ | ▭ | ▭ |
| **8** | ▭ | ▭ | ▭ | ▭ | ▭ | ▭ | ▭ | ▭ | ▭ | ▭ |
| **9** | ▭ | ▭ | ▭ | ▭ | ▭ | ▭ | ▭ | ▭ | ▭ | ▭ |
| **10** | ▭ | ▭ | ▭ | ▭ | ▭ | ▭ | ▭ | ▭ | ▭ | ▭ |

# EXERCISE 16:

**Instructions: For each question in the following passage, select the most appropriate word from the table below.**

| A. stand | B. withered | C. desired | D. father | E. sigh |
|----------|-------------|------------|-----------|---------|
| F. sickly | G. limbs | H. tumbled | I. dragging | J. looks |

It could not be said that the Prince missed his mother; children of his age cannot do that; but somehow, after she died everything seemed to go wrong with him. From a beautiful baby he became pale and [ 1 _____ ], seeming to have almost ceased growing, especially in his legs, which had been so fat and strong. But after the day of his christening they [ 2 _____ ], and when he was nearly a year old, and his nurse tried to make him stand, he only [ 3 _____ ] down.

This happened so many times that at last people began to talk about it. A prince, and not able to [ 4 _____ ] on his legs! What a misfortune to the country!

After a time he became stronger and his body grew, but his [ 5 _____ ] remained shrunken. No one talked of this to the King, for he was very sad.

The King [ 6 _____ ] that the Prince should keep the name given him by the

little old woman in grey and so he was known as Dolor.

Once a week, according to established state custom, the Prince, dressed in his very best, was

brought to the King, his [ 7 _____ ], for half an hour, but his Majesty was too

melancholy to pay much attention to the child.

Only once, when the King and his brother were sitting together, with Prince Dolor playing in

a corner of the room, [ 8 _____ ] himself about with his arms, rather than his

legs, it seemed to strike the father that all was not right with his son.

"How old is his Royal Highness?" said he, suddenly, to the nurse.

"Two years, three months, and five days, please your Majesty."

"It does not please me," said the King with a [ 9 _____ ]. "He ought to be far

more forward than he is. Is there not something wrong about him?"

"Oh, no," said the King's brother, exchanging meaning [ 10 _____ ] with the

nurse. "Nothing to make your Majesty at all uneasy. No doubt his Royal Highness will

outgrow it in time."

**Exercise 16 - Answer Sheet:**

| | A | B | C | D | E | F | G | H | I | J |
|---|---|---|---|---|---|---|---|---|---|---|
| **1** | A ▭ | B ▭ | C ▭ | D ▭ | E ▭ | F ▭ | G ▭ | H ▭ | I ▭ | J ▭ |
| **2** | A ▭ | B ▭ | C ▭ | D ▭ | E ▭ | F ▭ | G ▭ | H ▭ | I ▭ | J ▭ |
| **3** | A ▭ | B ▭ | C ▭ | D ▭ | E ▭ | F ▭ | G ▭ | H ▭ | I ▭ | J ▭ |
| **4** | A ▭ | B ▭ | C ▭ | D ▭ | E ▭ | F ▭ | G ▭ | H ▭ | I ▭ | J ▭ |
| **5** | A ▭ | B ▭ | C ▭ | D ▭ | E ▭ | F ▭ | G ▭ | H ▭ | I ▭ | J ▭ |
| **6** | A ▭ | B ▭ | C ▭ | D ▭ | E ▭ | F ▭ | G ▭ | H ▭ | I ▭ | J ▭ |
| **7** | A ▭ | B ▭ | C ▭ | D ▭ | E ▭ | F ▭ | G ▭ | H ▭ | I ▭ | J ▭ |
| **8** | A ▭ | B ▭ | C ▭ | D ▭ | E ▭ | F ▭ | G ▭ | H ▭ | I ▭ | J ▭ |
| **9** | A ▭ | B ▭ | C ▭ | D ▭ | E ▭ | F ▭ | G ▭ | H ▭ | I ▭ | J ▭ |
| **10** | A ▭ | B ▭ | C ▭ | D ▭ | E ▭ | F ▭ | G ▭ | H ▭ | I ▭ | J ▭ |

## EXERCISE 17:

**Instructions: For each question in the following passage, select the most appropriate word from the table below.**

| A. Prince | B. running | C. useless | D. denied | E. infant |
|-----------|-----------|-----------|-----------|-----------|
| F. sweetest | G. sweetest | H. children | I. doctors | J. shock |

(Continued from the previous exercise)

"Out-grow what?"

"A slight delicacy—ahem!—in the spine—something inherited, perhaps, from his dear mother."

"Ah, she was always delicate; but she was the [ **1** ] woman that ever lived. Come here, my little son."

The Prince turned to his father a small, sweet, grave face—like his mother's, and the King smiled and held out his arms. But when the boy came to him, not [ **2** ] like a boy, but wriggling awkwardly along the floor, the royal countenance clouded.

"I ought to have been told of this. Send for all the [ **3** ] in my kingdom immediately."

They came, and agreed in what had been pretty well known before; that the prince must

have been hurt when he was an **4** [          ]. Did anybody remember?

No, nobody. Indignantly, all the nurses **5** [          ] that any such accident had

happened.

But of all this the King knew nothing, for, indeed, after the first **6** [          ] of

finding out that his son could not walk, and seemed never likely to walk, he interfered very

little concerning him. He could not walk; his limbs were mere **7** [          ]

additions to his body, but the body itself was strong and sound, and his face was the same as

ever—just like his mother's face, one of the **8** [          ] in the world!

Even the King, indifferent as he was, sometimes looked at the little fellow with sad

tenderness, noticing how cleverly he learned to crawl, and swing himself about by his arms,

so that in his own awkward way he was as active as most **9** [          ] of his age.

"Poor little man! he does his best, and he is not unhappy," said the King to his brother. "I

have appointed you as Regent. In case of my death, you will take care of my poor little boy?"

Soon after he said this, the King died, as suddenly and quietly as the Queen had done, and

Prince Dolor was left without either father or mother—as sad a thing as could happen, even

to a **10** [          ].

## Exercise 17 - Answer Sheet:

| 1 | A ☐ | B ☐ | C ☐ | D ☐ | E ☐ | F ☐ | G ☐ | H ☐ | I ☐ | J ☐ |
|---|---|---|---|---|---|---|---|---|---|---|
| 2 | A ☐ | B ☐ | C ☐ | D ☐ | E ☐ | F ☐ | G ☐ | H ☐ | I ☐ | J ☐ |
| 3 | A ☐ | B ☐ | C ☐ | D ☐ | E ☐ | F ☐ | G ☐ | H ☐ | I ☐ | J ☐ |
| 4 | A ☐ | B ☐ | C ☐ | D ☐ | E ☐ | F ☐ | G ☐ | H ☐ | I ☐ | J ☐ |
| 5 | A ☐ | B ☐ | C ☐ | D ☐ | E ☐ | F ☐ | G ☐ | H ☐ | I ☐ | J ☐ |
| 6 | A ☐ | B ☐ | C ☐ | D ☐ | E ☐ | F ☐ | G ☐ | H ☐ | I ☐ | J ☐ |
| 7 | A ☐ | B ☐ | C ☐ | D ☐ | E ☐ | F ☐ | G ☐ | H ☐ | I ☐ | J ☐ |
| 8 | A ☐ | B ☐ | C ☐ | D ☐ | E ☐ | F ☐ | G ☐ | H ☐ | I ☐ | J ☐ |
| 9 | A ☐ | B ☐ | C ☐ | D ☐ | E ☐ | F ☐ | G ☐ | H ☐ | I ☐ | J ☐ |
| 10 | A ☐ | B ☐ | C ☐ | D ☐ | E ☐ | F ☐ | G ☐ | H ☐ | I ☐ | J ☐ |

## EXERCISE 18:

**Instructions: For each question in the following passage, select the most appropriate word from the table below.**

| A. | thronging | B. | cripple | C. | ridiculous | D. | majesty | E. | shouts |
|----|-----------|----|---------|----|-----------|----|---------|----|--------|
| F. | crown | G. | revived | H. | prepared | I. | seldom | J. | sucking |

He was more than that now, though. He was a king. In Nomansland as in other countries, the

people were struck with grief one day and ___**1**___ the next. "The king is

dead—long live the king!" was the cry that rang through the nation, and almost before his

late Majesty had been laid beside the queen, crowds came ___**2**___ from all

parts to the royal palace, eager to see the new monarch.

They did see him—sitting on the floor of the council-chamber, ___**3**___ his

thumb! And when one of the gentlemen-in-waiting lifted him up and carried him to the chair

of state, and put the ___**4**___ on his head, he shook it off again, it was so

heavy and uncomfortable. Sliding down to the foot of the throne, he began playing with the

gold lions that supported it;—laughing as if he had at last found something to amuse him.

"It is very unfortunate," said one of the lords. "It is always bad for a nation when its king is a

child; but such a child—a permanent ___**5**___ , if not worse."

"Let us hope not worse," said another lord in a very hopeless tone, and looking towards the Regent, who stood erect and pretended to hear nothing. "I have heard that these kind of children with very large heads and great broad foreheads and staring eyes, are—well, well, let us hope for the best and be [ **6** ___ ] for the worst. In the meantime—"

"Come forth and kiss the hilt of his sword," said the Regent—"I swear to perform my duties as Regent, to take care of his [ **7** ___ ] , and I shall do my humble best to govern the country."

Whenever the Regent and his sons appeared, they were received with [ **8** ___ ]

—"Long live the Regent!" "Long live the Royal family!"

As for the other child, his Royal Highness Prince Dolor—somehow people soon ceased to call him his Majesty, which seemed such a [ **9** ___ ] title for a poor little fellow, a helpless cripple, with only head and trunk, and no legs to speak of—he was seen very [ **10** ___ ] by anybody.

**Exercise 18 - Answer Sheet:**

| | A | B | C | D | E | F | G | H | I | J |
|---|---|---|---|---|---|---|---|---|---|---|
| **1** | A ▭ | B ▭ | C ▭ | D ▭ | E ▭ | F ▭ | G ▭ | H ▭ | I ▭ | J ▭ |
| **2** | A ▭ | B ▭ | C ▭ | D ▭ | E ▭ | F ▭ | G ▭ | H ▭ | I ▭ | J ▭ |
| **3** | A ▭ | B ▭ | C ▭ | D ▭ | E ▭ | F ▭ | G ▭ | H ▭ | I ▭ | J ▭ |
| **4** | A ▭ | B ▭ | C ▭ | D ▭ | E ▭ | F ▭ | G ▭ | H ▭ | I ▭ | J ▭ |
| **5** | A ▭ | B ▭ | C ▭ | D ▭ | E ▭ | F ▭ | G ▭ | H ▭ | I ▭ | J ▭ |
| **6** | A ▭ | B ▭ | C ▭ | D ▭ | E ▭ | F ▭ | G ▭ | H ▭ | I ▭ | J ▭ |
| **7** | A ▭ | B ▭ | C ▭ | D ▭ | E ▭ | F ▭ | G ▭ | H ▭ | I ▭ | J ▭ |
| **8** | A ▭ | B ▭ | C ▭ | D ▭ | E ▭ | F ▭ | G ▭ | H ▭ | I ▭ | J ▭ |
| **9** | A ▭ | B ▭ | C ▭ | D ▭ | E ▭ | F ▭ | G ▭ | H ▭ | I ▭ | J ▭ |
| **10** | A ▭ | B ▭ | C ▭ | D ▭ | E ▭ | F ▭ | G ▭ | H ▭ | I ▭ | J ▭ |

EXERCISE 19:

___

Instructions: For each question in the following passage, select the most appropriate word from the table below.

| A. mother | B. buried | C. better | D. surprise | E. familiar |
|-----------|-----------|-----------|-------------|-------------|
| F. noticed | G. live | H. resting | I. country | J. mourning |

(Continued from previous exercise)

Sometimes people daring to peer over the high wall of the palace garden [ 1 ___ ]

there a pretty little crippled boy with large dreamy, thoughtful eyes, beneath the grave

glance of which wrongdoers felt uneasy, and, although they did not know it then, the sight of

him bearing his affliction made them better.

If anybody had said that Prince Dolor's uncle was cruel, he would have said that what he did

was for the good of the [ 2 ___ ].

Therefore he went one day to the council-chamber, informed the ministers and the country

that the young King was in failing health, and that it would be best to send him for a time to

the Beautiful Mountains where his [ 3 ___ ] was born.

Soon after he obtained an order to send the King away—which was done in great state. The

nation learned, without much [ 4 ___ ], that the poor little Prince—had fallen ill on the road and died within a few hours; so declared the physician in attendance,

and the nurse who had been sent to take care of him. They brought the coffin back in great

state, and [ **5** ] him with his parents.

The country went into deep [ **6** ] for him, and then forgot him, and his

uncle reigned in his stead.

And what of the little lame prince, whom everybody seemed so easily to have forgotten?

Not everybody. There were a few kind souls, mothers of families, who had heard his sad

story, and some servants about the palace, who had been [ **7** ] with his

sweet ways—these many a time sighed and said, "Poor Prince Dolor!" Or, looking at the

Beautiful Mountains, which were visible all over Nomansland, though few people ever visited

them, "Well, perhaps his Royal Highness is [ **8** ] where he is."

They did not know that beyond the mountains, between them and the sea, lay a tract of

country, level, barren, except for a short stunted grass, and here and there a patch of tiny

flowers. Not a bush—not a tree—not a [ **9** ] place for bird or beast in

that dreary plain. It was not a pleasant place to [ **10** ] .

**Exercise 19 - Answer Sheet:**

| | A | B | C | D | E | F | G | H | I | J |
|---|---|---|---|---|---|---|---|---|---|---|
| **1** | ▭ | ▭ | ▭ | ▭ | ▭ | ▭ | ▭ | ▭ | ▭ | ▭ |
| **2** | ▭ | ▭ | ▭ | ▭ | ▭ | ▭ | ▭ | ▭ | ▭ | ▭ |
| **3** | ▭ | ▭ | ▭ | ▭ | ▭ | ▭ | ▭ | ▭ | ▭ | ▭ |
| **4** | ▭ | ▭ | ▭ | ▭ | ▭ | ▭ | ▭ | ▭ | ▭ | ▭ |
| **5** | ▭ | ▭ | ▭ | ▭ | ▭ | ▭ | ▭ | ▭ | ▭ | ▭ |
| **6** | ▭ | ▭ | ▭ | ▭ | ▭ | ▭ | ▭ | ▭ | ▭ | ▭ |
| **7** | ▭ | ▭ | ▭ | ▭ | ▭ | ▭ | ▭ | ▭ | ▭ | ▭ |
| **8** | ▭ | ▭ | ▭ | ▭ | ▭ | ▭ | ▭ | ▭ | ▭ | ▭ |
| **9** | ▭ | ▭ | ▭ | ▭ | ▭ | ▭ | ▭ | ▭ | ▭ | ▭ |
| **10** | ▭ | ▭ | ▭ | ▭ | ▭ | ▭ | ▭ | ▭ | ▭ | ▭ |

## EXERCISE 20:

**Instructions: For each question in the following passage, select the most appropriate word from the table below.**

| A. clinging | B. present | C. utmost | D. pretence | E. stupid |
|---|---|---|---|---|
| F. rooms | G. saddle | H. desire | I. wicked | J. luxury |

(Continued from previous exercise)

It was a very great secret indeed, a state secret, which none but so clever a man as the

**1** [ ] king of Nomansland would ever have thought of. Within twenty feet

of the top, some ingenious architect had planned a perfect little house, divided into four

**2** [ ] . By making skylights, and a few slits in the walls for windows, and

raising a peaked roof which was hidden by the parapet, here was a dwelling complete; eighty

feet from the ground and hard to reach.

Inside it was furnished with all the comfort and elegance imaginable; with lots of books and

toys, and everything that the heart of a child could **3** [ ] .

One winter night, when all the plain was white with moonlight, there was seen crossing it, a

great tall, black horse, ridden by a man also big and equally black, carrying before him on the

**4** [ ] , a woman and a child. The sad fierce-looking woman was a criminal

Mastering 11+/Cloze – Book TWO/ashkraft educational

under sentence of death, but her sentence had been changed. She was to inhabit the lonely tower with the child; she was to live as long as the child lived—no longer. This, in order that she might take the [ **5** ] care of him; for those who put him there were equally afraid of his dying and of his living. And yet he was only a little gentle boy, with a sweet smile. He was very tired with his long journey and was [ **6** ] to the man's neck, for he was rather frightened.

The tired little boy was Prince Dolor. He was not dead at all. His grand funeral had been a [ **7** ] ; a wax figure having been put in his place, while he was spirited away by the condemned woman and the black man. The latter was deaf and dumb, so could tell nothing.

Prince Dolor had every [ **8** ] that even a Prince could need, and the one thing wanting—love, never having known, he did not miss. His nurse was very kind to him, though she was a [ **9** ] woman. Perhaps it made her better to be shut up with an innocent child. By-and-by he began to learn lessons—not that his nurse had been ordered to teach him, but she did it partly to amuse herself. She was not a stupid woman, and Prince Dolor was by no means a [ **10** ] child; so they got on very well.

**Exercise 20 - Answer Sheet:**

| | A | B | C | D | E | F | G | H | I | J |
|---|---|---|---|---|---|---|---|---|---|---|
| **1** | ☐ | ☐ | ☐ | ☐ | ☐ | ☐ | ☐ | ☐ | ☐ | ☐ |
| **2** | ☐ | ☐ | ☐ | ☐ | ☐ | ☐ | ☐ | ☐ | ☐ | ☐ |
| **3** | ☐ | ☐ | ☐ | ☐ | ☐ | ☐ | ☐ | ☐ | ☐ | ☐ |
| **4** | ☐ | ☐ | ☐ | ☐ | ☐ | ☐ | ☐ | ☐ | ☐ | ☐ |
| **5** | ☐ | ☐ | ☐ | ☐ | ☐ | ☐ | ☐ | ☐ | ☐ | ☐ |
| **6** | ☐ | ☐ | ☐ | ☐ | ☐ | ☐ | ☐ | ☐ | ☐ | ☐ |
| **7** | ☐ | ☐ | ☐ | ☐ | ☐ | ☐ | ☐ | ☐ | ☐ | ☐ |
| **8** | ☐ | ☐ | ☐ | ☐ | ☐ | ☐ | ☐ | ☐ | ☐ | ☐ |
| **9** | ☐ | ☐ | ☐ | ☐ | ☐ | ☐ | ☐ | ☐ | ☐ | ☐ |
| **10** | ☐ | ☐ | ☐ | ☐ | ☐ | ☐ | ☐ | ☐ | ☐ | ☐ |

# WORD SELECTION

# EXERCISE 21:

**Instructions: For each question in the following passage, select the most appropriate word from the options given.**

He was the most beautiful prince that ever was born.

Being a prince, people said this; and it was true. When he looked at the candle, his eyes had an earnest expression quite startling in a new-born baby. His nose was aquiline; his complexion was healthy; he was round, fat, and straight-limbed—a splendid baby.

His father and mother, King and Queen of Nomansland, and their

**1**  A ▭ subjects
B ▭ heirs
C ▭ artefacts

were proud and happy, having waited ten years for an heir. The only person not quite happy

was the king's brother, who would have been

**2**  A ▭ prisoner
B ▭ happy
C ▭ king

had the baby

not been born, but his Majesty was very kind to him, and gave him a Dukedom as large as a country.

The Prince's christening was to be a grand affair; there were chosen for him four and twenty

godfathers and godmothers, who each had to give him a name, and

**3**  A ▭ premise
B ▭ promise
C ▭ provide

to do their utmost for him. When he came of age, he himself had to choose the name—and

the godfather or godmother—that he liked **4**
A ⬜ best
B ⬜ worst
C ⬜ least
.

All was rejoicing and the rich gave dinners and feasts for the poor.

The only quiet place in the Palace was the room, which though the prince was six weeks old,

his mother, the Queen, had not quitted. Nobody thought she was ill as she said nothing

about it herself, but lay pale and placid, giving no **5**
A ⬜ trouble
B ⬜ illness
C ⬜ happiness
to anybody.

Christening day came at last and it was as lovely as the Prince himself. All the people in the

Palace were beautifully **6**
A ⬜ dressed
B ⬜ decorated
C ⬜ masked
in the clothes which the Queen

had given them.

By six in the morning all the royal household had dressed itself in its very best; and then the

little Prince was dressed in his magnificent christening robe; which he did not like at all, but

kicked and screamed like any **7**
A ⬜ special
B ⬜ sick
C ⬜ common
baby. When he had calmed down,

they carried him to the bed where the Queen lay. She kissed and blessed him, and then she

gave him up with a gentle smile, saying she "hoped he would be very good, that it would be a very nice christening, and all the guests would

**8**
A ☐ bemuse
B ☐ enjoy
C ☐ envy

themselves,"

and turned peacefully over on her bed. She was a very uncomplaining person—the Queen,

and her name was Dolorez.  Everything went on as if she had been present. All, even the King

himself, had grown used to her

**9**
A ☐ presence
B ☐ mannerisms
C ☐ absence

for she was not strong, and

for years had not joined in the gaieties. The noble company arrived from many countries;

also the four-and-twenty godfathers and godmothers, who had been chosen with care, as

the people who would be most

**10**
A ☐ useless
B ☐ awkward
C ☐ useful

to his Royal Highness

should he ever want friends.

---

**Answer Sheet:**

| 1 | A ☐ | B ☐ | C ☐ | 6 | A ☐ | B ☐ | C ☐ |
|---|---|---|---|---|---|---|---|
| 2 | A ☐ | B ☐ | C ☐ | 7 | A ☐ | B ☐ | C ☐ |
| 3 | A ☐ | B ☐ | C ☐ | 8 | A ☐ | B ☐ | C ☐ |
| 4 | A ☐ | B ☐ | C ☐ | 9 | A ☐ | B ☐ | C ☐ |
| 5 | A ☐ | B ☐ | C ☐ | 10 | A ☐ | B ☐ | C ☐ |

## EXERCISE 22:

**Instructions: For each question in the following passage, select the most appropriate word from the options given.**

(Continued from previous exercise)

They came, walking two and two, with their coronets on their **1**
- A ☐ heads
- B ☐ hands —
- C ☐ backs

dukes and duchesses, princes and princesses; they all kissed the child and pronounced the

name which each had given him. Then the four-and-twenty names were shouted out, one

after another, and **2**
- A ☐ struck
- B ☐ written
- C ☐ read

down, to be kept in the state records.

Everybody was satisfied except the little Prince, who moaned faintly under his christening

robes, which nearly smothered him.

Though very few knew it, the Prince in coming to the chapel had met with an accident. A

young lady of rank, whose **3**
- A ☐ account
- B ☐ means
- C ☐ duty

it was to carry him to and from

the chapel, had been so busy arranging her train with one hand, that she stumbled and let

him **4**
- A ☐ fail
- B ☐ fall
- C ☐ file

. She picked him up—the accident was so slight it seemed

hardly worth speaking of. The baby had turned pale, but did not cry. No one knew that

anything was wrong. Even if he had moaned, the silver trumpets were loud enough to drown

his **5**
A ⬜ voice
B ⬜ vice
C ⬜ laughter
. It would have been a pity to let anything trouble such a

day.

Such a procession! Heralds in blue and silver; pages in crimson and gold; and a troop of little

girls in dazzling white, **6**
A ⬜ trying
B ⬜ carrying
C ⬜ dancing
baskets of flowers, which they strewed

all the way before the child and the nurse,—finally the four and twenty godfathers and

godmothers, splendid to look at.

The prince was a mere heap of lace and muslin, and had it not been for a canopy of white

satin and ostrich feathers, which was held over him whenever he was carried, his presence

would have been **7**
A ⬜ glorified
B ⬜ verified
C ⬜ unnoticed
.

"It is just like fairyland," said one little flower-girl to another, "and I think the only thing the

Prince wants now is a fairy godmother."

"Does he?" said a shrill, but soft and not unpleasant voice, and a person no larger than a

child was seen.

She was a pleasant little, old, grey-haired, grey-eyed woman,

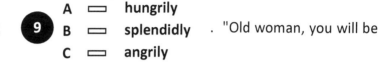

| 8 | A | ▭ | dressed |
|---|---|---|---|
|   | B | ▭ | soiled |
|   | C | ▭ | drenched |

all in grey.

"Take care and don't let the baby fall again."

The grand nurse started, flushing

| 9 | A | ▭ | hungrily |
|---|---|---|---|
|   | B | ▭ | splendidly |
|   | C | ▭ | angrily |

. "Old woman, you will be

kind enough not to say, 'the baby,' but 'the Prince.' Keep away; his Royal Highness is just

going to sleep."

| 10 | A | ▭ | must |
|----|---|---|---|
|    | B | ▭ | wish |
|    | C | ▭ | just |

"I ... kiss him, I am his godmother."

---

**Answer Sheet:**

| 1 | A ▭ | B ▭ | C ▭ | | 6 | A ▭ | B ▭ | C ▭ |
|---|-----|-----|-----|---|---|-----|-----|-----|
| 2 | A ▭ | B ▭ | C ▭ | | 7 | A ▭ | B ▭ | C ▭ |
| 3 | A ▭ | B ▭ | C ▭ | | 8 | A ▭ | B ▭ | C ▭ |
| 4 | A ▭ | B ▭ | C ▭ | | 9 | A ▭ | B ▭ | C ▭ |
| 5 | A ▭ | B ▭ | C ▭ | | 10 | A ▭ | B ▭ | C ▭ |

**Instructions: For each question in the following passage, select the most appropriate word from the options given.**

The sun was shining so brightly through the foremost windows of the old schoolhouse in

Upper Wood, that the children of the first and second classes appeared as if covered with

gold. They looked at one another, all with beaming faces, partly because the sun made them

appear so, and **1** A ▭ paltry / B ▭ partial / C ▭ partly    for joy; for when the sunshine came through the

last window, then the moment approached that the closing word would be spoken, and the

children could rush out into the evening sunshine. The teacher was still busy with the

illuminated heads of the second class, and indeed with some zeal, for several sentences had

still to be **2** A ▭ compiled / B ▭ completed / C ▭ contemplated   , before the school could be closed. The teacher

was standing before a boy who looked well-fed and quite comfortable, and who was looking

up into the teacher's face with eyes as **3** A ▭ square / B ▭ bright / C ▭ round   as two little balls.

"Well, Ritz, hurry, you surely must have thought of something by now. Now then! What can

be made useful in a household? Do not forget to mention the three indispensable qualities of the object."

Ritz, the youngest son of the minister, was usually busy thinking of that which had just

happened to him. So just now it had come to his **(4)**

| A | mind |
|---|------|
| B | brain |
| C | soul |

, how this

very morning Auntie had arrived. She was an older sister of his mother and had no home of

her own; but made a home with her relatives. She was a **(5)**

| A | fervent |
|---|---------|
| B | frivolous |
| C | frequent |

visitor

at the parsonage for months at a time and would help the mother in governing the

household.  Ritz remembered especially, that Auntie was particularly inclined to have the

children go to bed in good time and they had to go; and he also **(6)**

| A | remained |
|---|----------|
| B | remembered |
| C | refrained |

that they could not get the extra ten minutes from Mother, for Auntie was always against

begging Mother. In fact, Auntie talked so much about going to bed, that Ritz felt the feared

command of retiring during the whole day. So his thoughts were occupied with these

experiences, and he said after some **(7)**

| A | thinking |
|---|----------|
| B | thoughts |
| C | thing |

: "One can make

use of an aunt in a household. She must—she must—she must—"

"Well, what must she? That will be something different from a quality," the teacher

interrupted the laborious speech of the boy.

"She must not always be reminding that it is time to go to bed," it now came out.

"Ritz," the teacher said now in a **8** A ☐ severe / B ☐ serial / C ☐ several tone, "is the school the

place to joke?"   But Ritz looked at the teacher with such unmistakable fright and

astonishment, that the latter saw that it was an honest opinion which Ritz had made use of

in his sentence. He therefore changed his mind and said more **9** A ☐ gently / B ☐ severely : / C ☐ louder

"Your sentence is unfitting and incorrect, for your three qualities are not  there. Do you

understand that, Ritz? You will have to make three sentences at home, all alike; but do not

forget the different qualities. Have you **10** A ☐ understated / B ☐ understand / C ☐ understood me?"

---

**Answer Sheet:**

| | A | B | C | | | A | B | C |
|---|---|---|---|---|---|---|---|---|
| **1** | A ☐ | B ☐ | C ☐ | | **6** | A ☐ | B ☐ | C ☐ |
| **2** | A ☐ | B ☐ | C ☐ | | **7** | A ☐ | B ☐ | C ☐ |
| **3** | A ☐ | B ☐ | C ☐ | | **8** | A ☐ | B ☐ | C ☐ |
| **4** | A ☐ | B ☐ | C ☐ | | **9** | A ☐ | B ☐ | C ☐ |
| **5** | A ☐ | B ☐ | C ☐ | | **10** | A ☐ | B ☐ | C ☐ |

**Instructions: For each question in the following passage, select the most appropriate word from the options given.**

The friendly village Upper Wood lay on the top of the hill close by the fir wood; it had a

beautiful white church with a high, slender tower. At a

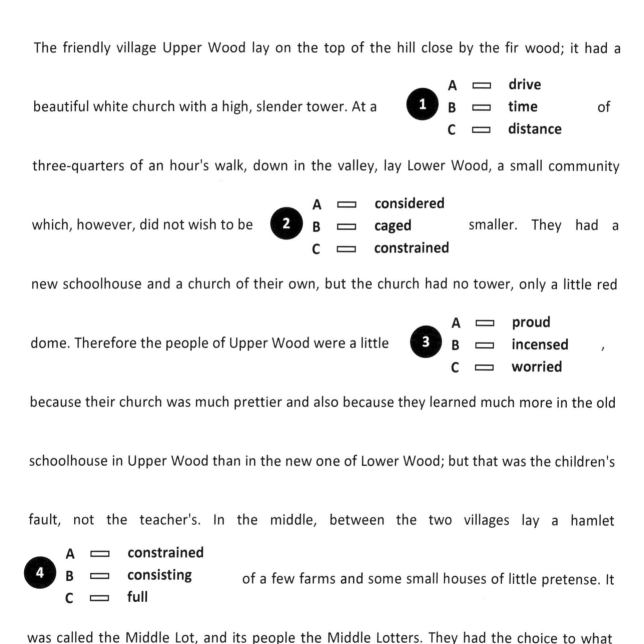

**1**
A ☐ drive
B ☐ time
C ☐ distance

of

three-quarters of an hour's walk, down in the valley, lay Lower Wood, a small community

which, however, did not wish to be

**2**
A ☐ considered
B ☐ caged
C ☐ constrained

smaller. They had a

new schoolhouse and a church of their own, but the church had no tower, only a little red

dome. Therefore the people of Upper Wood were a little

**3**
A ☐ proud
B ☐ incensed
C ☐ worried

,

because their church was much prettier and also because they learned much more in the old

schoolhouse in Upper Wood than in the new one of Lower Wood; but that was the children's

fault, not the teacher's. In the middle, between the two villages lay a hamlet

**4**
A ☐ constrained
B ☐ consisting
C ☐ full

of a few farms and some small houses of little pretense. It

was called the Middle Lot, and its people the Middle Lotters. They had the choice to what

church and school they wished to belong, whether to Lower Wood or Upper Wood, and according to their choice they were judged by the people of Upper Wood; for whoever

wanted to learn much and be decent, he must, according to the Upper Wooders, strive to

**5**
- A ☐ belong
- B ☐ defect
- C ☐ despise

to them. This was a fixed and general idea of the people on the

top of the hill. In the Middle Lot there lived only two families who were generally respected;

the Justice of Peace, who was obliged to **6**
- A ☐ leave
- B ☐ live
- C ☐ like

there because otherwise he

would have to be called there, and that would have been inconvenient. This peace-making

man was Kaetheli's father. And the other was old Marianne, who lived in her own house and

pulled horse-hair for a living, and never did harm to anyone.

When on the next morning the three children of the parsonage **7**
- A ☐ pierced
- B ☐ looked
- C ☐ passed

Marianne's house on their way to school, Sally said: "It is fun to go to school to-day for the

strange boy of yesterday will come too; if we only knew his name. Kaetheli described him to

me; he wears velvet pants. Of course he will come to Upper Wood to school."

"Of course," said Edi with a **8**
- A ☐ dignified
- B ☐ smelly
- C ☐ malicious

air; "who would think of going to

Lower Wood to School?"

Mastering 11+/Cloze – Book TWO/ashkraft educational

"Of course, who would go there to school?" observed Ritz.

Then the three in perfect harmony  the schoolhouse.

9
A ▭ ebbed
B ▭ cornered
C ▭ entered

But no strange face was to be seen in the whole schoolroom; everything went on in the usual

way to the end of the morning. Then everyone hurried away in different directions. Sally was

standing there, somewhat undecided; she would like to have heard something new of the

10
A ▭ strong
B ▭ scary
C ▭ strange

boy and his mother, for she loved to hear news, and now not

even Kaetheli, with whom she talked things over, had been in school.

---

**Answer Sheet:**

| 1 | A ▭ | B ▭ | C ▭ | | 6 | A ▭ | B ▭ | C ▭ |
|---|---|---|---|---|---|---|---|---|
| 2 | A ▭ | B ▭ | C ▭ | | 7 | A ▭ | B ▭ | C ▭ |
| 3 | A ▭ | B ▭ | C ▭ | | 8 | A ▭ | B ▭ | C ▭ |
| 4 | A ▭ | B ▭ | C ▭ | | 9 | A ▭ | B ▭ | C ▭ |
| 5 | A ▭ | B ▭ | C ▭ | | 10 | A ▭ | B ▭ | C ▭ |

# EXERCISE 25:

**Instructions: For each question in the following passage, select the most appropriate word from the options given.**

SQUIRE TRELAWNEY, Dr. Livesey, and the rest of these gentlemen having asked me to write

down the whole particulars about Treasure Island, from the **1**
- A ▭ begin
- B ▭ inception
- C ▭ beginning
to

the end, keeping nothing back but the bearings of the island, and that only because there is

still treasure not yet lifted, I take up my pen in the year of grace 17__ and go back to the

**2**
- A ▭ time
- B ▭ place
- C ▭ treasure
when my father kept the Admiral Benbow inn and the brown old

seaman with the sabre cut first took up his lodging under our roof.

I remember him as if it were **3**
- A ▭ yesterday
- B ▭ never
- C ▭ tomorrow
, as he came plodding to the inn

door, his sea-chest following behind him in a hand-barrow—a tall, strong, heavy, nut-brown

man, his tarry pigtail falling over the shoulder of his soiled blue coat, his hands ragged and

scarred, with black, broken nails, and the sabre cut across one cheek, a dirty, livid white. I

**4**
- A ▭ reminded
- B ▭ remember
- C ▭ remanded
him looking round the cover and whistling to himself as he did

so, and then breaking out in that old sea-song that he sang so often afterwards:

*"Fifteen men on the dead man's chest—*

*Yo-ho-ho, and a bottle of rum!"*

in the high, old tottering (5)

| | | |
|---|---|---|
| A | ▭ | **voice** |
| B | ▭ | **blare** |
| C | ▭ | **noise** |

that seemed to have been tuned

and broken at the capstan bars. Then he rapped on the door with a bit of stick like a

handspike that he carried, and when my father appeared, called roughly for a glass of rum.

This, when it was brought to him, he drank slowly, like a connoisseur, lingering on the taste

and still looking about him at the cliffs and up at our signboard.

"This is a handy cove," says he at length; "and a pleasant sittyated grog-shop. Much

company, mate?"

My father told him no, very little (6)

| | | |
|---|---|---|
| A | ▭ | **company** |
| B | ▭ | **customs** |
| C | ▭ | **singing** |

the more was the pity.

"Well, then," said he, "this is the berth for me. Here you, matey," he cried to the man who

trundled the barrow; "bring up alongside and help up my chest. I'll stay here a bit," he

continued. "I'm a plain man; rum and (7)

| | | |
|---|---|---|
| A | ▭ | **beacon** |
| B | ▭ | **baton** |
| C | ▭ | **bacon** |

and eggs is what I

want, and that head up there for to watch ships off. What you mought call me? You mought call me captain. Oh, I see what you're at—there"; and he threw down three or four gold

pieces on the threshold. "You can tell me when I've worked
 
**8**
A ☐ thorough
B ☐ threw
C ☐ through

that," says he, looking as fierce as a commander.

And indeed bad as his clothes were and coarsely as he spoke, he had none of the

**9**
A ☐ appearance
B ☐ niceties
C ☐ logic
of a man who sailed before the mast, but seemed like a mate

or skipper accustomed to be obeyed or to
 
**10**
A ☐ strike
B ☐ pound
C ☐ spend
.

---

**Answer Sheet:**

| 1 | A ☐ | B ☐ | C ☐ | | 6 | A ☐ | B ☐ | C ☐ |
|---|---|---|---|---|---|---|---|---|
| 2 | A ☐ | B ☐ | C ☐ | | 7 | A ☐ | B ☐ | C ☐ |
| 3 | A ☐ | B ☐ | C ☐ | | 8 | A ☐ | B ☐ | C ☐ |
| 4 | A ☐ | B ☐ | C ☐ | | 9 | A ☐ | B ☐ | C ☐ |
| 5 | A ☐ | B ☐ | C ☐ | | 10 | A ☐ | B ☐ | C ☐ |

# EXERCISE 26:

**Instructions: For each question in the following passage, select the most appropriate word from the options given.**

(Continued from previous exercise)

He was a very silent man by custom. All day he hung round the cove or upon the cliffs with a

brass telescope; all evening he sat in a corner of the parlour next the fire and drank rum and

water very strong. Mostly he would not **1**
- A ⬜ speak
- B ⬜ judge
- C ⬜ smile

when spoken to,

only look up sudden and fierce and blow through his nose like a fog-horn; and we and the

people who came about our house soon **2**
- A ⬜ learned
- B ⬜ sought
- C ⬜ brought

to let him be. Every

day when he came back from his stroll he would ask if any seafaring men had gone by along

the road. At first we thought it was the **3**
- A ⬜ want
- B ⬜ surplus
- C ⬜ excess

of company of his own

kind that made him ask this question, but at last we began to see he was desirous to avoid

them. When a seaman did put up at the Admiral Benbow (as now and then some did, making

by the coast road for Bristol) he would look in at him through the curtained door before he

**4**
- A ⬜ enter
- B ⬜ entry
- C ⬜ entered

the parlour; and he was always sure to be as silent as a

mouse when any such was present. For me, at least, there was no secret about the matter, for I was, in a way, a sharer in his alarms. He had taken me aside one day and promised me a

silver fourpenny on the first of every month if I would only keep my "weather-eye

**5**
A ▭ closed
B ▭ open          for a seafaring man with one leg" and let him know the
C ▭ blinked

moment he appeared. Often enough when the first of the month came round and I applied

to him for my wage, he would only blow through his nose at me and stare me down, but

before the week was out he was sure to think better of it, bring me my four-penny piece, and

**6**
A ▭ retreat
B ▭ repeat          his orders to look out for "the seafaring man with one
C ▭ rejoice

leg."

How that personage haunted my dreams, I need scarcely tell you. On stormy nights, when

the wind shook the four corners of the house and the surf roared along the cove and up the

cliffs, I would see him in a thousand forms, and with a thousand diabolical expressions. Now

the leg would be cut off at the knee, now at the hip; now he was a monstrous kind of a

creature who had never had but the one     **7**
A ▭ eye
B ▭ leg          , and that in the middle
C ▭ hand

of his body. To see him leap and run and pursue me over hedge and ditch was the worst of nightmares. And altogether I paid pretty dear for my

8
A ☐ weekly
B ☐ daily
C ☐ monthly

fourpenny

piece, in the shape of these abominable fancies.

But though I was so

9
A ☐ confident
B ☐ terrified
C ☐ undaunted

by the idea of the seafaring man

with one leg, I was far less afraid of the captain himself than anybody else who knew him.

There were nights when he took a deal more rum and water than his head would carry; and

then he would sometimes sit and sing his wicked, old, wild sea-songs, minding nobody; but

sometimes he would call for glasses round and force all the trembling company to listen to

his stories or bear a

10
A ☐ chorus
B ☐ chant
C ☐ carol

to his singing.

**Answer Sheet:**

| 1 | A ☐ | B ☐ | C ☐ | 6 | A ☐ | B ☐ | C ☐ |
|---|---|---|---|---|---|---|---|
| 2 | A ☐ | B ☐ | C ☐ | 7 | A ☐ | B ☐ | C ☐ |
| 3 | A ☐ | B ☐ | C ☐ | 8 | A ☐ | B ☐ | C ☐ |
| 4 | A ☐ | B ☐ | C ☐ | 9 | A ☐ | B ☐ | C ☐ |
| 5 | A ☐ | B ☐ | C ☐ | 10 | A ☐ | B ☐ | C ☐ |

## EXERCISE 27:

**Instructions: For each question in the following passage, select the most appropriate word from the options given.**

(Continued from previous exercise)

ABOUT noon I stopped at the captain's door with some cooling drinks and medicines. He was

lying very much as we had **1** 
A ☐ left
B ☐ borrowed
C ☐ exiled
him, only a little higher, and he

seemed both weak and excited.

"Jim," he said, "you're the only one here that's worth anything, and you know I've been

always good to you. Never a month **2** 
A ☐ and
B ☐ every
C ☐ but
I've given you a silver

fourpenny for yourself. And now you see, mate, I'm pretty low, and deserted by all; and Jim,

you'll bring me one noggin of rum, now, won't you, matey?"

"The doctor—" I began.

But he broke in cursing the doctor, in a **3** 
A ☐ ferocious
B ☐ robust
C ☐ feeble
voice but heartily.

"Doctors is all swabs," he said; "and that doctor there, why, what do he know about

seafaring men? I been in places hot as pitch, and mates dropping round with Yellow Jack, and the blessed land a-heaving like the sea with earthquakes—what to the doctor know of lands

like that?—and I lived on rum, I tell you. It's been meat and drink, and man and wife, to me;

and if I'm not to have my **4**
- A ☐ meat
- B ☐ rum
- C ☐ medicine

now I'm a poor old hulk on a lee

shore, my blood'll be on you, Jim, and that doctor swab"; and he ran on again for a while

with **5**
- A ☐ curses
- B ☐ blessings
- C ☐ songs

. "Look, Jim, how my fingers fidges," he continued in the

pleading tone. "I can't keep 'em still, not I. I haven't had a drop this blessed day. That

doctor's a **6**
- A ☐ genius
- B ☐ fool
- C ☐ sage

, I tell you. If I don't have a drain o' rum, Jim, I'll

have the horrors; I seen some on 'em already. I seen old Flint in the corner there, behind

you; as plain as print, I seen him; and if I get the horrors, I'm a man that has lived rough, and

I'll raise Cain. Your doctor hisself said one glass wouldn't **7**
- A ☐ benefit
- B ☐ hurt
- C ☐ satisfy

me. I'll give you a golden guinea for a noggin, Jim."

He was growing more and more excited, and this alarmed me for my father, who was very

low that day and needed **8**
- A ☐ quite
- B ☐ quite
- C ☐ quiet

; besides, I was reassured by the doctor's

words, now quoted to me, and rather offended by the offer of a bribe.

"I want none of your

- A ⬜ money
- **9** B ⬜ stories
- C ⬜ lies

," said I, "but what you owe my father. I'll

get you one glass, and no more."

When I brought it to him, he

- A ⬜ passed
- **10** B ⬜ seized
- C ⬜ conferred

it greedily and drank it out.

"Aye, aye," said he, "that's some better, sure enough. And now, matey, did that doctor say

how long I was to lie here in this old berth?"

"A week at least," said I.

---

**Answer Sheet:**

| | A | B | C | | | A | B | C |
|---|---|---|---|---|---|---|---|---|
| **1** | A ⬜ | B ⬜ | C ⬜ | | **6** | A ⬜ | B ⬜ | C ⬜ |
| **2** | A ⬜ | B ⬜ | C ⬜ | | **7** | A ⬜ | B ⬜ | C ⬜ |
| **3** | A ⬜ | B ⬜ | C ⬜ | | **8** | A ⬜ | B ⬜ | C ⬜ |
| **4** | A ⬜ | B ⬜ | C ⬜ | | **9** | A ⬜ | B ⬜ | C ⬜ |
| **5** | A ⬜ | B ⬜ | C ⬜ | | **10** | A ⬜ | B ⬜ | C ⬜ |

# EXERCISE 28:

**Instructions: For each question in the following passage, select the most appropriate word from the options given.**

Four-and-thirty years ago, Bob Ainslie and I were coming up Infirmary Street from the High

School, our heads together, and our arms intertwisted, as only lovers and boys know

how, or
**1**
A ▭ who
B ▭ when
C ▭ why

.

When we got to the top of the street, and turned north, we espied a crowd at the Tron

Church. "A dog-fight!" shouted Bob, and was off; and so was I, both of us all but praying that

it might not be over
**2**
A ▭ before
B ▭ after
C ▭ since
we got up! And is not this boy-nature? and

human nature too? and don't we all wish a house on fire not to be out before we see it?

Dogs like fighting; old Isaac says they "delight" in it, and for the best of all reasons; and boys

are not cruel because they like to see the
**3**
A ▭ fire
B ▭ fight
C ▭ house
. They see three of

the great cardinal virtues of dog or man—courage, endurance, and skill—in intense action.

This is very different from a love of making dogs fight, and enjoying, and aggravating, and

making gain by their pluck. A boy,—be he ever so fond himself of fighting,—if he be a good boy, hates and

**4**
- A ⬜ despises
- B ⬜ likes
- C ⬜ admires

all this, but he would have run off with

Bob and me fast enough: it is a natural, and a not wicked interest, that all boys and men have

in witnessing intense energy in action.

Does any curious and finely-ignorant woman wish to know how Bob's eye at a glance

announced a dog-fight to his brain? He did not, he could not, see the dogs fighting: it was a

flash of an inference, a rapid induction. The

**5**
- A ⬜ host
- B ⬜ crowd
- C ⬜ congregation

round    a

couple of dogs fighting is a crowd masculine mainly, with an occasional active,

compassionate

**6**
- A ⬜ man
- B ⬜ woman
- C ⬜ dog

fluttering wildly round the outside and using her

tongue and her hands freely upon the men, as so many "brutes;" it is a crowd annular,

compact, and mobile; a crowd centripetal, having its eyes and its heads all bent downwards

and inwards, to one common focus.

Well, Bob and I are up, and find it is not over: a small thoroughbred white bull terrier is busy

throttling a large shepherd's dog, unaccustomed to war, but not to be trifled with. They are

hard at it; the scientific little fellow doing his work in great style, his pastoral enemy fighting wildly, but with the sharpest of teeth and a great courage. Science and breeding, however,

soon had their own; the Game Chicken, as the premature Bob called him, working his way

up, took his final grip of poor Yarrow's throat,—and he lay

**7**
A ☐ gasping
B ☐ energising
C ☐ puffing

and done for. His master, a brown, handsome, big young shepherd from Tweedsmuir, would

have liked to have knocked down any man, would "drink up Esil, or eat a crocodile," for that

part, if he had a chance: it was no use kicking the little dog; that would only make him hold

the closer. Many were the means

**8**
A ☐ murmured
B ☐ whispered
C ☐ shouted

out in mouthfuls, of

the best possible ways of ending it. "Water!" but there was none near, and many cried for it

who might have got it from the well at Blackfriar's Wynd. "Bite the tail!" and a large, vague,

benevolent, middle-aged man, more desirous than wise, with some struggle got the bushy

end of Yarrow's tail into his ample mouth, and bit it with all his

**9**
A ☐ might
B ☐ sight
C ☐ trifle

.

This was more than enough for the much-enduring, much-perspiring shepherd, who, with a

gleam of

**10**
A ☐ joy
B ☐ sorrow
C ☐ grief

over his broad visage, delivered a terrific facer upon our

large, vague, benevolent, middle-aged friend,—who went down like a shot.

**Answer Sheet:**

| | A | B | C | | | A | B | C |
|---|---|---|---|---|---|---|---|---|
| **1** | ⬜ | ⬜ | ⬜ | | **6** | ⬜ | ⬜ | ⬜ |
| **2** | ⬜ | ⬜ | ⬜ | | **7** | ⬜ | ⬜ | ⬜ |
| **3** | ⬜ | ⬜ | ⬜ | | **8** | ⬜ | ⬜ | ⬜ |
| **4** | ⬜ | ⬜ | ⬜ | | **9** | ⬜ | ⬜ | ⬜ |
| **5** | ⬜ | ⬜ | ⬜ | | **10** | ⬜ | ⬜ | ⬜ |

**Mastering 11+/Cloze – Book TWO/ashkraft educational**

# EXERCISE 29:

**Instructions: For each question in the following passage, select the most appropriate word from the options given.**

I was now beginning to grow handsome; my coat had grown fine and soft, and was bright

black. I had one white foot and a pretty white star on my forehead. I was thought very

handsome; my **1**    A ▭ **master**    B ▭ **helper**    C ▭ **servant**    would not sell me till I was four years old; he

said lads ought not to work like men, and colts ought not to work like horses till they were

quite **2**    A ▭ **grown**    B ▭ **sewn**    C ▭ **went**    up.

When I was four years old Squire Gordon came to look at me. He examined my eyes, my

mouth, and my legs; he felt them all down; and then I had to walk and trot and gallop before

him. He seemed to like me, and said, "When he has been well broken in he will do very well."

My master said he would break me in himself, as he should not like me to be frightened or

hurt, and he lost no time about it, for the next day he **3**    A ▭ **began**    B ▭ **halted**    C ▭ **stopped**    .

Every one may not know what breaking in is, therefore I will describe it. It means to teach a horse to wear a saddle and bridle, and to carry on his back a man, **4** A ☐ women B ☐ woman C ☐ child or

child; to go just the way they wish, and to go quietly. Besides this he has to learn to wear a

collar, a crupper, and a breeching, and to stand still while they are put on; then to have a cart

or a chaise fixed behind, so that he cannot walk or trot without dragging it after him; and he

must go fast or slow, just as his driver **5** A ☐ wishes B ☐ abhors C ☐ loathes . He must never start at

what he sees, nor speak to other horses, nor bite, nor kick, nor have any will of his own; but

always do his master's will, even though he may be very tired or hungry; but the worst of all

is, when his harness is once on, he may neither jump for joy nor lie down for

**6** A ☐ vigour B ☐ drive C ☐ weariness . So you see this breaking in is a great thing.

I had of course long been used to a halter and a headstall, and to be led about in the fields

and lanes quietly, but now I was to have a bit and bridle; my master gave me some oats as

usual, and after a good deal of coaxing he got the bit into my mouth, and the bridle fixed, but

it was a nasty thing! Those who have never had a bit in their **7** A ☐ ears B ☐ mouths C ☐ eyes

cannot think how bad it feels; a great piece of cold hard steel as thick as a man's finger to be

pushed into one's mouth, between one's teeth, and over one's tongue, with the ends coming out at the corner of your mouth, and held fast there by straps over your head, under your

throat, round your nose, and under your chin; so that no way in the world can you get

8
A ▭ rid
B ▭ bound
C ▭ chained

of the nasty hard thing; it is very bad! yes, very bad! at least I

thought so; but I knew my mother always wore one when she went out, and all horses did

when they were grown up; and so, what with the nice oats, and what with my master's pats,

9
A ▭ wear
B ▭ writ
C ▭ ware

kind words, and gentle ways, I got to my bit and bridle.   Next

came the saddle, but that was not half so bad; my master put it on my back very gently,

while old Daniel held my head; he then made the girths fast under my body, patting and

talking to me all the time; then I had a few oats, then a little leading about; and this he did

10
A ▭ burden
B ▭ bridle
C ▭ saddle

every day till I began to look for the oats and the .

**Answer Sheet:**

| 1 | A ▭ | B ▭ | C ▭ | | 6 | A ▭ | B ▭ | C ▭ |
|---|-----|-----|-----|---|---|-----|-----|-----|
| 2 | A ▭ | B ▭ | C ▭ | | 7 | A ▭ | B ▭ | C ▭ |
| 3 | A ▭ | B ▭ | C ▭ | | 8 | A ▭ | B ▭ | C ▭ |
| 4 | A ▭ | B ▭ | C ▭ | | 9 | A ▭ | B ▭ | C ▭ |
| 5 | A ▭ | B ▭ | C ▭ | | 10 | A ▭ | B ▭ | C ▭ |

# EXERCISE 30:

**Instructions: For each question in the following passage, select the most appropriate word from the options given.**

(Continued from previous exercise)

One morning, my master got on my back and rode me round the **1**

| | | |
|---|---|---|
| A | ▭ | meadow |
| B | ▭ | head |
| C | ▭ | river |

on the soft grass. It certainly did feel queer; but I must say I felt rather proud to

carry my master, and as he continued to ride me a little every day I soon became

**2**

| | | |
|---|---|---|
| A | ▭ | ignorant |
| B | ▭ | Ill-mannered |
| C | ▭ | accustomed |

to it.

The next unpleasant business was putting on the iron shoes; that too was very hard at first.

My master went with me to the smith's forge, to see that I was not **3**

| | | |
|---|---|---|
| A | ▭ | hurt |
| B | ▭ | coarse |
| C | ▭ | bored |

or got any fright. The blacksmith took my feet in his hand, one after the other, and cut away

some of the hoof. It did not pain me, so I stood still on three legs till he had done them all.

Then he took a piece of iron the shape of my foot, and clapped it on, and drove some nails

through the shoe quite into my hoof, so that the shoe was **4**

| | | |
|---|---|---|
| A | ▭ | unevenly |
| B | ▭ | firmly |
| C | ▭ | insecurely |

on.

My feet felt very stiff and heavy, but in time I got used to it.

And now having got so far, my master went on to break me to harness; there were more

new things to wear. First, a stiff heavy collar just on my neck, and a bridle with great side-

pieces against my eyes called blinkers, and blinkers indeed they were, for I could not see on

either side, but only  **5**  A ☐ **straight**  in front of me; next, there was a
                            B ☐ **square**
                            C ☐ **level**

small saddle with a nasty stiff strap that went right under my tail; that was the crupper. I

hated the crupper; to have my long tail doubled up and poked through that strap was almost

as bad as the bit. I never felt more like kicking, but of course I could not kick such a good

**6**  A ☐ **bit**
      B ☐ **crupper**   , and so in time I got used to everything, and could do my work
      C ☐ **master**

as well as my mother.

I must not forget to mention one part of my training, which I have always considered a very

great advantage. My master sent me for a fortnight to a neighboring farmer's, who had a

meadow which was skirted on one side by the railway. Here were some sheep and cows, and

I was turned in  **7**  A ☐ **against**  them.
                       B ☐ **abroad**
                       C ☐ **among**

I shall never forget the first train that ran by. I was feeding quietly near the pales which separated the meadow from the railway, when I heard a strange sound at a distance, and

before I knew whence it came—with a rush and a clatter, and a ⑧

A ⬜ puffing
B ⬜ huffing
C ⬜ chuffing

out of smoke—a long black train of something flew by, and was gone almost before I could

draw my breath. I turned and galloped to the further side of the meadow as fast as I could

go, and there I stood snorting with astonishment and fear. In the course of the day many

other trains went by, some more slowly; these drew up at the station close by, and

sometimes made an awful shriek and groan before they ⑨

A ⬜ moved
B ⬜ stopped
C ⬜ checked

. I

thought it very dreadful, but the cows went on eating very quietly, and hardly raised their

⑩
A ⬜ tails
B ⬜ heads
C ⬜ feet

as the black frightful thing came puffing and grinding past.

---

**Answer Sheet:**

| 1 | A ⬜ | B ⬜ | C ⬜ | | 6 | A ⬜ | B ⬜ | C ⬜ |
|---|---|---|---|---|---|---|---|---|
| 2 | A ⬜ | B ⬜ | C ⬜ | | 7 | A ⬜ | B ⬜ | C ⬜ |
| 3 | A ⬜ | B ⬜ | C ⬜ | | 8 | A ⬜ | B ⬜ | C ⬜ |
| 4 | A ⬜ | B ⬜ | C ⬜ | | 9 | A ⬜ | B ⬜ | C ⬜ |
| 5 | A ⬜ | B ⬜ | C ⬜ | | 10 | A ⬜ | B ⬜ | C ⬜ |

# ANSWERS

Please check www.mastering11plus.com/answers for answers and
additional answer sheets.

Email enquiry@mastering11plus.com for any feedback or
clarification on the answers

# ANSWERS:

| EXERCISE 1 Cloze | | EXERCISE 2 Cloze | | EXERCISE 3 Cloze | | EXERCISE 4 Cloze | | EXERCISE 5 Cloze | |
|---|---|---|---|---|---|---|---|---|---|
| 1 | A | 1 | D | 1 | A | 1 | C | 1 | G |
| 2 | G | 2 | A | 2 | H | 2 | J | 2 | J |
| 3 | E | 3 | G | 3 | G | 3 | E | 3 | I |
| 4 | J | 4 | F | 4 | C | 4 | A | 4 | B |
| 5 | B | 5 | C | 5 | E | 5 | F | 5 | H |
| 6 | F | 6 | H | 6 | F | 6 | D | 6 | F |
| 7 | C | 7 | B | 7 | J | 7 | H | 7 | E |
| 8 | I | 8 | E | 8 | D | 8 | I | 8 | C |
| 9 | H | 9 | J | 9 | I | 9 | B | 9 | D |
| 10 | D | 10 | I | 10 | B | 10 | G | 10 | A |

# ANSWERS:

| EXERCISE 6 Cloze | | EXERCISE 7 Cloze | | EXERCISE 8 Cloze | | EXERCISE 9 Cloze | | EXERCISE 10 Cloze | |
|---|---|---|---|---|---|---|---|---|---|
| 1 | G | 1 | F | 1 | F | 1 | G | 1 | A |
| 2 | D | 2 | J | 2 | I | 2 | J | 2 | C |
| 3 | F | 3 | A | 3 | B | 3 | A | 3 | E |
| 4 | B | 4 | G | 4 | C | 4 | I | 4 | F |
| 5 | C | 5 | H | 5 | D | 5 | E | 5 | J |
| 6 | I | 6 | D | 6 | J | 6 | B | 6 | H |
| 7 | A | 7 | B | 7 | G | 7 | H | 7 | D |
| 8 | H | 8 | I | 8 | H | 8 | F | 8 | I |
| 9 | E | 9 | C | 9 | A | 9 | C | 9 | B |
| 10 | J | 10 | E | 10 | E | 10 | D | 10 | G |

# ANSWERS:

| EXERCISE 11 Cloze | | EXERCISE 12 Cloze | | EXERCISE 13 Cloze | | EXERCISE 14 Cloze | | EXERCISE 15 Cloze | |
|---|---|---|---|---|---|---|---|---|---|
| 1 | C | 1 | A | 1 | B | 1 | A | 1 | A |
| 2 | I | 2 | I | 2 | E | 2 | D | 2 | B |
| 3 | B | 3 | J | 3 | F | 3 | B | 3 | F |
| 4 | F | 4 | H | 4 | D | 4 | E | 4 | G |
| 5 | G | 5 | F | 5 | J | 5 | G | 5 | C |
| 6 | H | 6 | D | 6 | G | 6 | F | 6 | H |
| 7 | E | 7 | C | 7 | H | 7 | H | 7 | D |
| 8 | D | 8 | B | 8 | I | 8 | I | 8 | I |
| 9 | J | 9 | G | 9 | A | 9 | C | 9 | E |
| 10 | A | 10 | E | 10 | C | 10 | J | 10 | J |

# ANSWERS:

| EXERCISE 16 Cloze | | EXERCISE 17 Cloze | | EXERCISE 18 Cloze | | EXERCISE 19 Cloze | | EXERCISE 20 Cloze | |
|---|---|---|---|---|---|---|---|---|---|
| 1 | F | 1 | G | 1 | G | 1 | F | 1 | B |
| 2 | B | 2 | B | 2 | A | 2 | I | 2 | F |
| 3 | H | 3 | I | 3 | J | 3 | A | 3 | H |
| 4 | A | 4 | E | 4 | F | 4 | D | 4 | G |
| 5 | G | 5 | D | 5 | B | 5 | B | 5 | C |
| 6 | C | 6 | J | 6 | H | 6 | J | 6 | A |
| 7 | D | 7 | C | 7 | D | 7 | E | 7 | D |
| 8 | I | 8 | F | 8 | E | 8 | C | 8 | J |
| 9 | E | 9 | H | 9 | C | 9 | H | 9 | I |
| 10 | J | 10 | A | 10 | I | 10 | G | 10 | E |

# ANSWERS:

| EXERCISE 21 Cloze | | EXERCISE 22 Cloze | | EXERCISE 23 Cloze | | EXERCISE 24 Cloze | | EXERCISE 25 Cloze | |
|---|---|---|---|---|---|---|---|---|---|
| 1 | A | 1 | A | 1 | C | 1 | C | 1 | C |
| 2 | C | 2 | B | 2 | B | 2 | A | 2 | A |
| 3 | B | 3 | C | 3 | C | 3 | A | 3 | A |
| 4 | A | 4 | B | 4 | A | 4 | B | 4 | B |
| 5 | A | 5 | A | 5 | C | 5 | A | 5 | A |
| 6 | A | 6 | B | 6 | B | 6 | B | 6 | A |
| 7 | C | 7 | C | 7 | A | 7 | C | 7 | C |
| 8 | B | 8 | A | 8 | A | 8 | A | 8 | C |
| 9 | C | 9 | c | 9 | A | 9 | C | 9 | A |
| 10 | C | 10 | A | 10 | C | 10 | C | 10 | C |

# ANSWERS:

| EXERCISE 26 Cloze | | EXERCISE 27 Cloze | | EXERCISE 28 Cloze | | EXERCISE 29 Cloze | | EXERCISE 30 Cloze | |
|---|---|---|---|---|---|---|---|---|---|
| 1 | A | 1 | A | 1 | C | 1 | A | 1 | A |
| 2 | A | 2 | C | 2 | A | 2 | A | 2 | C |
| 3 | A | 3 | C | 3 | B | 3 | A | 3 | A |
| 4 | C | 4 | B | 4 | A | 4 | B | 4 | B |
| 5 | B | 5 | A | 5 | B | 5 | A | 5 | A |
| 6 | B | 6 | B | 6 | B | 6 | C | 6 | C |
| 7 | B | 7 | B | 7 | A | 7 | B | 7 | C |
| 8 | C | 8 | C | 8 | c | 8 | A | 8 | A |
| 9 | B | 9 | A | 9 | A | 9 | A | 9 | B |
| 10 | A | 10 | B | 10 | A | 10 | C | 10 | B |

# Other books in the **Mastering 11+** series:

- ➢ English & Verbal Reasoning – Practice Book 1
- ➢ English & Verbal Reasoning – Practice Book 2
- ➢ English & Verbal Reasoning – Practice Book 3

- ➢ Cloze Tests – Practice Book 1
- ➢ Cloze Tests – Practice Book 3

- ➢ Maths – Practice Book 1
- ➢ Maths – Practice Book 2
- ➢ Maths – Practice Book 3

- ➢ Comprehension – Multiple Choice Exercise Book 1
- ➢ Comprehension – Multiple Choice Exercise Book 2
- ➢ Comprehension – Multiple Choice Exercise Book 3

- ➢ CEM Practice Papers – Pack 1
- ➢ CEM Practice Papers – Pack 2
- ➢ CEM Practice Papers – Pack 3
- ➢ CEM Practice Papers – Pack 4

- ➢ Mastering 11+ Vocabulary

All queries to **enquiry@mastering11plus.com**

10969302R00062

Printed in Great Britain
by Amazon.co.uk, Ltd.,
Marston Gate.